A Guided Inquiry Approach
to High School Research

A Guided Inquiry Approach to High School Research

Randell K. Schmidt

Libraries Unlimited Guided Inquiry

LIBRARIES UNLIMITED

AN IMPRINT OF ABC-CLIO, LLC
Santa Barbara, California • Denver, Colorado • Oxford, England

Library of Congress Cataloging-in-Publication Data

Schmidt, Randell K.
  A guided inquiry approach to high school research / Randell K. Schmidt.
      pages cm. — (Libraries Unlimited guided inquiry)
  Includes bibliographical references and index.
  ISBN 978-1-61069-287-8 (pbk.) — ISBN 978-1-61069-288-5 (ebook)
  1. Research—Methodology—Study and teaching (Secondary)—United States. 2. Report writing—Study and teaching (Secondary)—United States. 3. Information literacy—Study and teaching (Secondary)—United States.
4. School librarian participation in curriculum planning—United States. 5. Teaching teams—United States.
I. Title.
  LB1047.3.S36 2013
  373.1'3044—dc23   2012042818

ISBN: 978-1-61069-287-8
EISBN: 978-1-61069-288-5

17 16 15 14 13   1 2 3 4 5

This book is also available on the World Wide Web as an eBook.
Visit www.abc-clio.com for details.

Libraries Unlimited
An Imprint of ABC-CLIO, LLC

ABC-CLIO, LLC
130 Cremona Drive, P.O. Box 1911
Santa Barbara, California 93116-1911

This book is printed on acid-free paper ∞
Manufactured in the United States of America

*This book is dedicated to all those ninth grade students at Gill St. Bernard's
whose intelligence, stamina, and good humor
contributed to the materials found within.*

*And to Joseph & Olivia,
Geoffrey & Ybelka
and
Gabriel Ulysses.*

Contents

Foreword

One of the most challenging times in a child's life is the transition from primary and middle school to high school. How does the child shift from being an elementary school student to learning to be a secondary school scholar? This is the time when students often become confused about what is expected of them and lost in not knowing where to go for help. The purpose of this book is to provide guidance for students to become successful high school scholars. The book is full of practical ways to guide students toward academic success and college readiness.

A Guided Inquiry Approach to High School Research is part of the Guided Inquiry series that is based on my research on students' process of learning from a variety of sources that is described in the Information Search Process (ISP). ISP describes seven evolving stages in students' thoughts, feelings, and actions in the process of learning through inquiry. *Guided Inquiry: Learning in the 21st Century* (Kuhlthau, Maniotes, & Caspari, 2007) is the foundational text in this series.

In my two decades on the faculty at Rutgers University as director of the School Library Specialization in the master's degree program, I had the pleasure of teaching many talented students. Randell Schmidt was one of the most outstanding. One day after strongly urging students to put the ISP into practice to improve learning in their schools, I cautioned, "The task will not be easy. You may find it difficult to change research assignments to inquiry learning with the traditional mind set so engrained." Randi responded, "I will do it!" And she did. Randi's efforts became a model of the powerful impact inquiry learning has on an entire school. Gill St. Bernard School became a working lab for our research at the Center for International Scholarship in School Libraries at Rutgers.

Randi's workshops in this book have been developed, tested with students, reworked, and refined to provide guidance in each stage of the ISP. Important research skills and information literacy are integrated at the time of need. Research assignments are drawn into school class time as a way of learning rather than as extra homework. This time-tested approach has been extremely effective and gradually became an integral part of the school program. Students going through the program find that they have made the transition to high school scholars. Graduates report that this is a critical part of their high school education that prepared them for college work. This addition to the Guided Inquiry series is a practical manual for developing high school scholars and is a companion to Schmidt's first book, *Lessons for a Scientific Literature Review: Guiding the Inquiry*.

Carol Collier Kuhlthau, Professor Emerita
Rutgers, The State University of New Jersey

Preface

Academic success and college readiness are among the goals of most high school curricula. The answer to the question of how to reach those goals differs in every high school in the country. However, a consensus is building that high school students should learn how to find and handle information in depth, interacting with multiple formats and sources of information as they respond to a need to know.

This consensus is built upon the recognition that no high school can teach as much knowledge as is expected but that every high school can teach students to find, process, and think about new information to synthesize into their own knowledge.

This book describes a high school curriculum that instructs the fundamentals of scholarly research, while using a nontraditional approach to the research question. The book introduces students to an Information Search Process (ISP) (Kuhlthau, 2004), which allows the choosing of whatever topic he/she wants to learn about—whether that topic is atomic energy, ice cream, or zookeeping—and guides the student on an inquiry journey.

Usually, the young high school student possesses little background knowledge of the topic. Therefore, the inquiry does not begin with a thesis statement, as the student's knowledge base is not extensive enough. Instead, the inquiry may well be an inarticulated question. For example, the student wants to know about the Cuban Missile Crisis but cannot initially express what it is he wants to know. He does not have the informational background to ask a clear question.

The inquiry he makes may be as simple as, "I am interested in the Cuban Missile Crisis." Therefore, his first question can be stated as, "What can I find out about the Cuban Missile Crisis?" Such an inquiry can be guided by the teacher and librarian in collaboration. They will introduce lessons on information finding, assessment, and integration. All of their lessons culminate in a series of steps toward a presentation of whatever the student has found and learned in his research. As such, his presentation is the report of his research findings. It is neither an argument, an essay, nor a proof. Rather, it presents an array of information, creatively produced for public consumption, of the student's research. Therefore, the unifying idea of the presentation is not created by an articulated, essential question but by what the student has found and how he has decided to present what he has found. Above all, the project is dependent upon the curiosity in the student's mind, not upon a list of research topics introduced by the teachers.

The responsibility for the student's inquiry is shared by the student and the Teaching Team, which consists of a teacher, librarian, and one other adult who is a research aide or a content expert. The irony here is that the ISP produces an eventual reversal of roles, as the Teaching Team guides the student researcher to gain more and more information, and eventually, some knowledge or expertise that no one on the Teaching Team possesses.

We teachers and librarians become like Socrates, who is described by social philosopher James P. Carse in his book, *Breakfast at the Victory* (1994, p. 69):

What we see in Socrates is not a developed philosophy but an engaged receptivity, an active listening. If there is anything resembling a method here it is his attempt to raise insight in his students of which he himself was incapable. In other words, Socrates' originality consists in his ability to originate in others what he could not originate in himself.

Acknowledgments

While it may not take a village to write a book, nonetheless, it does take a community to teach a class of high school students the broad and finer points of academic rigor and protocol. This community over the past dozen years includes administrators, fellow teachers, sister librarians, and all of the ninth grade students who have traveled through the library's Research and Writing program. Everyone has either knowingly or unknowingly contributed to the depth and refinements of the curriculum found herein.

Special thanks go to Barbara Ripton, English Department chair, who contributed to the scaffolded design of the syllabus and project and to the note-taking lesson; Virginia Kowalski who co-taught the curriculum with me for several years and helped solidify some of the lessons; Claudia Hesler who created the database lessons and maintains the library operations during the many weeks each year that I teach almost every class period and who creates the presentation's annual program schedule; and Peter Schmidt whose leadership over several years as the high school principal mandated and supported a course requirement in scholarly research to prepare all students for the 21st century.

The book you are reading would not have been possible without the assistance, knowledgeable input, and skills added by my former student and intern who is now a colleague, Courtney Puglisi. Courtney urged me to start and finish the book and provided layout assistance, content, and criticism as well as processing the manuscript. Courtney also developed the assignment timeline. In many ways, this book is her work as well as mine.

In addition, my son Geoffrey Schmidt, a public high school teacher in New York City, has assisted me in aligning the Common Core Curriculum Standards matched to and noted within each workshop session plan. His articulation of differentiations of student behavior noted within some workshops was instructive and particularly appreciated. I could not have written the book without Courtney and Geoffrey.

Heartfelt thanks go to all my past co-teachers including Laura Wengel, Andy Lutz, Karen Blair, and Derek Martin and to current co-teachers, Carrie Grabowski, Margery Schiesswohl, Amy Tierney, and Paul Canada, all of whom have contributed materials or comments within the text. Thanks also to former intern, Josephine Muench, whose scholarship in adolescent cognition has aided my work with students. Additional thanks to former librarian colleagues Mary Fran Daley, Anne Rosenthal, and Maureen Smyth for help in developing lessons on browsing, searching, and handling information.

Quietly working behind the scenes to receive permissions, complete the references, and assist with the social network information was former student and colleague Emilia Giordano and editorial wonder woman Cecilia Rhodes. Teacher Kathy Maisano of Maryland and librarian Cynthia Washburn of New Jersey have been generous in their manuscript criticism. I thank them.

Thanks go also to Goran Brolund of Uppsala, Sweden, whose expertise in guided inquiry helped to shape the book contents. Scholarly observations and commentary from the faculty of Rutgers University over the years have included those from Dr. Carol Gordon and Dr. Ross Todd as well as several MLIS and PhD students who have assisted with teaching or studying the curriculum.

My editor Sharon Coatney has once again provided timely and invaluable assistance while cheerfully shepherding the manuscript preparation. I am in your debt, Sharon.

The book, and indeed, the curriculum would not be a reality were it not for my good fortune in being a student and later mentee of Dr. Carol Kuhlthau whose groundbreaking conception of the "Information Search Process" caught my imagination so many years ago and whose past as well as current work (with co-authors Leslie Maniotes and Anne Caspari) provided the compass by which I have guided my students and steered my work. Thank you, Carol.

Teacher's Practicum

Introduction to Teacher's Practicum

The 22 workshops found in this book have been developed, evaluated, and refined over the past 12 years, during which the Research and Writing Project has been taught at a small, independent high school in New Jersey. The initial 10 workshops were modeled after the Information Search Process (ISP) described by Professor Carol Kuhlthau in her book *Seeking Meaning* (2004), and the lessons were designed to accommodate the student researchers' feelings, thoughts, and actions, which Kuhlthau described in her model.

Our Research and Writing Project was developed to introduce new high school students to the concept of research in a scholarly manner so students could learn to find information, synthesize it for meaning, and present it to peers and teachers. As the years passed and available information sources grew, older workshops were refined and newer workshops were added (such as the workshop on public and private language and the effects of social media upon public and private language).

From the first, we have called our class-times *workshops*, maintaining an older child-centric interactive emphasis upon the student as inquirer and the teacher as guide.

Since its inception, we have insisted upon a team-teaching approach, recognizing that guided inquiry is a labor-intensive, collaborative effort in which a teacher, a librarian, and another adult resource person together can reach and guide a classroom full of excited learners. In our experience, the third adult resource brings additional expertise, needed people power, and often one-on-one assistance when a student is in need of inquiry intervention.

Note to Teachers:

This book is simply an effort to decode and simplify the basic high school research project. While the materials of this book were designed as a complete unit of guided inquiry curriculum, individual lessons may certainly be used on their own. Such lessons as research note taking, understanding perspective and bias, and using formal language while understanding the difference between private and public language can all be considered standalone lessons or workshop sessions.

The author's intention is to provide an educational framework to shift the paradigm of student learning from primary and middle school student to high school scholar. Such

a shift can be made as a whole curriculum or incrementally adapted by employing individual workshops.

Finally, the curriculum was originally designed for 14-year-old freshmen in a college-preparatory school. Such students in the modern high school setting are often overscheduled, overtired, and stressed out. The workshop format is designed to counter those three evils. Our aim is for students to recapture the joy and fulfillment of learning about something that interests the student. While the curriculum was designed as a ninth grade project, it is quite adaptable to other, higher grade levels and can be employed whether students do or do not have previous experience with guided inquiry for research projects. Our method is to guide the student into researching a topic in which the student has high interest and little knowledge so that the student's inquiry drives the research and provides the motivation necessary to complete the project. The book is a step-by-step manual for both the teacher/guide and student/scholar.

How to Save a Failed Project

Occasionally a child will experience a failed project. Such failure comes in different forms. In one recent class of 78 students, teachers witnessed four failed projects.

The first two failed projects were experienced by two girls who both came to the teachers and librarian at the end of Week 8 after they had judged their notes and determined they needed more information. One student was researching the FBI, the other was researching 20th-Century Fashion. Each student individually indicated she was tired of the topic and did not have the interest or the heart to continue. What should she do? After determining that both girls had done the appropriate work up to that point, each was consulted privately and asked if another topic was already chosen. Each girl indicated yes; one chose "dogs," the other chose "Marilyn Monroe." Both students were informed that they had one week, including the three-day holiday weekend, to catch up with their peers. Each was asked if she thought she could catch up. Each agreed and was given permission to switch topics. The assistant librarian was consulted to help locate sources quickly, and both girls caught up within a week.

A third failed project involved a student who did not "buy in" to the project from the beginning. Arriving late to class, complaining about the lessons, protesting the note-taking process, he was unhappy. Although a highly intelligent student, this project was not his cup of tea. He just wanted to do the research in the same way he had completed his eighth grade research at another school. For the teachers, his was a perplexing case. How could we get him on board? We conferred and decided to have him meet with all of us—librarian, teacher, and two library interns—so that we could ask him how we could help him get through the process to his satisfaction. The teacher also conferred with his mother. Slowly, the boy seemed to soften his stance and participate more happily. In the end, his presentation on boxing was voted "best presentation" by his peers.

A final failure, and perhaps the most potentially difficult case of the four examples, was of a ninth grade girl who realized her completed notes would not make an interesting speech and her audience would be bored. The intern who was checking student research notes on the Friday prior to the next Monday lesson on "How to Write Your Presentation Notes" came to me to report that the student was on the verge of tears. What should be done? When the librarian approached the student, she confirmed that her notes were not going to be interesting to her audience even though she was very interested in her chosen topic of "weddings." She did not want to give her speech. As tears welled up she said, "Maybe I should have researched something else."

At two weeks before presentations, researching something else was not an option. Asked to list her subtopics (she had an overabundance of note cards) she indicated that wedding dresses was one of her subtopics.

A brainstorm hit! She could focus on wedding dresses. Did she have time during the coming weekend to research Kate Middleton's dress and Kim Kardashian's dress? She did. Good. She could use her cards and add information about the two dresses, retitling her presentation: "The Royal and the Raunchy Wedding Dress." Tears disappeared; a smile came to her face. The failed project had been saved. She would borrow a teacher's wedding dress and wear it as realia for her presentation. She would present her research standing in front of the school's former chapel building. The project was saved!

Stitching Together Borrowed Information into a Research Quilt

Most young researchers do not initially understand how a research presentation or paper can be likened to a homemade quilt. As a matter of fact, many young researchers do not even understand what a pieced or patchwork quilt is, so the analogy of a research presentation to a quilt goes nowhere.

But with some illustrations of Amish (Pennsylvania Dutch) or African American quilts in hand, the concept of a pieced quilt, made by hand from small scraps of different pieces of material obtained from many sources, gains meaning. The student observes pictures of beautiful, well-pieced, functional quilts and begins to see that different pieces of fabric are brought together to complete a whole, unique design. Students are reminded to ask their elders about family quilts when possible.

In much the same way as a quilter makes a quilt by carefully piecing together different small scraps of material, creating a big picture or design, so, too, can a young researcher piece together small notes of borrowed information from several different information sources to design a whole new picture of his/her research topic.

This analogy allows a student to visualize the culmination of information gathering (scholarship) as the basis for borrowed information (scholarly) presentations. In other words, the student is creating his/her own research quilt, borrowing information bits here and knowledge scraps there and piecing them together in a design of his/her own choice. The design becomes the student's own organization of borrowed information, stitched together with his/her own experiences and new understandings of the research subject.

Certainly a presentation, just like a quilt, has its own particular design and does not cover everything. But like a quilt, a presentation shows off the bits and pieces of materials found and used to make it.

Researchers cannot (especially for a short project) cover all the information available on the topic. But like a quilt, research can highlight and display the unity of the topic through a variety of pieces of information borrowed from others for use in the presentation. The researcher stitches together the pieces and makes sense of different sources by creating a new, self-generated presentation or paper. A quilt of new knowledge has been made.

Assessments of the Research and Writing Project

Five assessments are employed for the Research and Writing Project:

1. Note cards and other elements of the project totaling 160 points as listed in the syllabus.
2. The presentation itself, which, although considered an element of the research project, comes under greater scrutiny.
3. The three instruments of the School Library Impact Measure (SLIM), developed by Rutgers University Professors Todd, Kuhlthau, and Heinstrom (2005) and the progression of the student's involvement with and knowledge of the topic.
4. The research file, its organization, contents, and continuity.
5. The student's efforts as a researcher.

Each assessment has its own parameters and values, so each will be described individually. First, however, the underlying philosophy of assessing the project should be explained, as it deviates from standard high school assessments for a key reason.

What is essentially being taught here is a method for learning by using the highly regarded, well-documented Information Search Process (ISP). It is accurate to say that we are *not* teaching for the final product—a good presentation. Instead we are teaching a process.

The presentation is really secondary. Our goal is to teach an information search process—the process of learning how to decide upon a topic, access information, identify further a more narrow topic, gather more resources, assimilate the information through synthesis with prior knowledge and experiences, create a presentation, and share the information formally, afterwards reflecting on what was learned.

The execution of the ISP is considered a lifelong skill set that will be used throughout the student's academic career and into his/her adult working and nonworking life. As such, our aim is for full participation in the ISP. Students cannot understand what they do not participate in.

Because this project introduces the ISP, we hold no illusions that in 12 weeks students will master a lifelong skill, just as we would not expect older students to quickly master and excel in other lifelong skills such as, cooking, sailing, or child rearing.

Therefore, our assessments focus not on the product but on the involvement of the student in the information search process.

The five assessments are described below:

1. The assessment of note cards is based upon: 1) the number of note cards made; 2) the requirement that each card be written in one to three full sentences; 3) whether each card is only about one idea; 4) that the cards hold valid, understandable information; 5) that each card has an author notation, source, and page number listed in the format we have taught the students; 6) that quotation statements be indicated with quote marks and noted as such; 7) that all other borrowed information notes be in the student's own words; and 8) that because this is a research project, *all* research notes will be made from borrowed information.
2. The presentation is judged by rotating teachers who follow a basic rubric. (See Appendix H for presentation rubric).

3. The instruments are part of an assessment package (SLIM) to gauge the accumulation of knowledge and the involvement in research by students as they experience the Information Search Process. Administered at the points when: 1) the student first decides upon a topic, 2) in the middle of the research note-taking task, and 3) after presentations have been completed, the three instruments are examined for the progression of knowledge accumulation and responses to that knowledge as reflected in the answers of the students.

4. Teachers examine the research file for organization of information collected and for handouts and notes kept. The file is likened to a suitcase of souvenirs of the student's research journey. Teachers are checking for content organization and completion. Evidence of printouts of research materials being read and notes being made, as well as all hand-outs and teachers' written instructions, must be held and organized in the research file.

5. The students' effort grade is counted as 20 percent of the entire grade. Unlike the other components, the effort assessment is more subjective and indicates not only how enthusiastically or positively the student responded to fulfilling requirements but also whether the student participated fully with his/her study buddy and inquiry group. Our experience has been to meet as a teaching team, examine the student's file and instruments and then discuss our own individual observations of the student's continued participation, assigning a numerical valuation to each student's effort.

Kuhlthau's Information Search Process (ISP)

The ISP discussed by Kuhlthau is a research-based, distinct model of information-seeking behaviors including feelings, thoughts, and actions manifest in the behaviors of a broad spectrum of information seekers (those people who are doing some form of long or short term research).

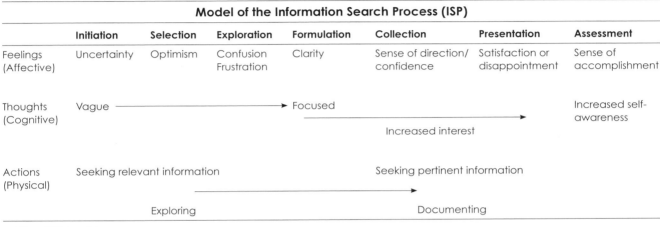

Model of the Information Search Process (ISP)

	Initiation	Selection	Exploration	Formulation	Collection	Presentation	Assessment
Feelings (Affective)	Uncertainty	Optimism	Confusion Frustration	Clarity	Sense of direction/ confidence	Satisfaction or disappointment	Sense of accomplishment
Thoughts (Cognitive)	Vague ──────────────────→ Focused				Increased interest		Increased self-awareness
Actions (Physical)	Seeking relevant information		Exploring		Seeking pertinent information	Documenting	

Kuhlthau (2004, p. 82)

The ISP model has since been employed by Kuhlthau, Maniotes, and Caspari (2007) as the theoretical basis for the Guided Inquiry, which is described in their book Guided Inquiry: Learning in the 21st Century.

Student Workshops

Research in the Initiation Stage of the Information Search Process

Workshop 1: The Assignment
Workshop 2: What Is the Information Search Process (ISP) and What Is Peer Review?
Workshop 3: Understanding Perspective and Bias in Information Sources
Workshop 4: What Are Learning Styles?
Workshop 5: Descriptive Essay of Your Learning Style

The Teaching Team for the 22 structured workshops will include three educational guides. They are: the content or classroom teacher, the librarian, and a third resource who will be either a teacher's aide or a content expert (resource guide) depending upon the particular workshop being conducted.

While the Initiation Stage contains five workshops, the teacher and librarian are encouraged to allow other additional unstructured class workshop times, particularly after the syllabus has been distributed and the active involvement of each student has begun. Students need time to examine introductory materials from specialized encyclopedias, guides, and manuals in the reference section. Students may wish to employ a Google search or discuss possibilities with other students, teachers, or librarians. In-class readings of materials, video viewing, photographic content viewing, or interaction with a content teacher should be permitted as students dip their toes into a research process.

The roles of librarian and teacher include field guide in the library, reference guide for the initial materials, and, perhaps most importantly, time management guide as the adults circulate among the new scholars to help them stay on task and not waste valuable academic time.

There are seven stages of the Information Search Process, from initiation through evaluation. Three forms of experience accompany each stage: 1) feelings about the project, 2) thoughts about the information, and 3) activities undertaken while researching information. The students now begin the first stage: Initiation.

Workshop 1: The Assignment

Overview

Introduction to a Guided Inquiry or How to Become a High School Scholar

The goal of this introductory workshop is for the student to understand the excitement and importance of learning how to do basic research with a guided inquiry method and an organized approach. Such research will improve the student's ability to succeed in the modern academic environment. In today's high schools, information is the raw material of knowledge building. Research skills are the tools needed in high school to handle that information. The student develops an inquiry when he/she identifies a topic, accesses information to develop a question about the topic, determines if the information is of good quality and use, interrogates the information through reading or observations, analyzes the information, and synthesizes the information to find meaning by connecting it to prior knowledge or experience. Thus the student comes to a new understanding of the topic through the research process. Once the process of research reaches the point of synthesis, the student must learn how to present new knowledge gained to share with others.

Before the research and writing assignment is given in the form of a syllabus, the student should be informed that a guided inquiry project is a community affair and that the student will be an explorer in the wilderness of information—a traveler searching for information to satisfy an inquiry—but the student will not be alone. Traveling with the student are the teacher and the librarian. Another teacher, teacher's aide, or community-based person who may be an expert in the topic being researched will also help. The student traveler then has fellow travelers who will guide and assist in the journey of the student's inquiry.

Other students in the class will be making similar journeys through the information wilderness to research and find material for their own presentations. They too, will have teacher and librarian guides.

And soon, the student will be paired with another student—a study buddy who will at several points during the information search process review the student's work and provide peer-to-peer feedback. Again the student will not be alone in the journey of inquiry. A study buddy will help by brainstorming, listening, sharing ideas, and providing another perspective on the student's research.

At different times throughout the research, the student and study buddy will join with one or two other sets of student/study buddy pairs in an inquiry group to share, provide feedback, discuss, and plan each student's inquiry and presentation.

The Assignment, a.k.a. the Syllabus

High school is the place where students engage in a process of learning the "stuff" that society wants the young adult to know. In some courses each assignment is about learning a small piece of knowledge that eventually accumulates to become a small body of knowledge about science or the humanities. The goal of this workshop is to familiarize the student researchers with the assignment and the concept that research is a process, and the research assignment in their hands—the syllabus for the research and writing project—outlines the plan to guide them through the research process.

Unlike most of the student's high school assignments, this assignment will last for 12 weeks and almost all the work will be done in class in a workshop format with help always available. The assignment has many parts, and much is expected of the student. But because this is a high school–level assignment, the student receives the syllabus at the beginning of the project. The student should not be intimidated by the expectations of teachers to fulfill the project requirements, but be reassured that although a large amount of work is expected of the student, almost all of it will take place during class time in a workshop and with an end point (the presentation) in sight.

High school students are notoriously overscheduled with sports, community service, jobs, and extracurricular activities. Students and their parents are more comfortable knowing of significant academic expectations early in the semester. The research and writing project is one such significant expectation.

An important note to the teachers:

Be aware that our syllabus is always—from year to year—a work in progress. Due dates, time, and requirements allotted for each portion of the project change based upon feedback from current students. For example, time allotted for note taking has been expanded upon the request of students, and the number of note cards has been decreased (again, after students' comments). Student assessments of the project are made at the end of the project and serve as planning tools to refine and revise the syllabus from year to year.

Workshop 1: The Assignment

Learning Goals: The goal of this workshop is to introduce the assignment.
Location: Library
Team: Teacher, Librarian, and Resource Guide
Inquiry Unit: This workshop shall provide an introduction to a guided, inquiry-based research project using the syllabus as an example of a plan for learning scholarly research.
Total Time: 50 minutes

Starter Time: 15 minutes Inquiry Community	Begin the class with a plate of cookies, explaining to the students that they will be rewarded with cookies at different points during the process. Show printed programs from previous year for a few minutes and ask students to think about the following (see Appendix E): 1. Why is there such a wide variety of topics? 2. Which of these presentations would you like to have seen? 3. What topic would you have liked to research? 4. Why did research have to be completed in order to give the presentation? 5. Could you give a five-minute presentation right now?
Worktime Time: 30 minutes Inquiry Community	Provide the students with the handout. Students remain in the inquiry community as the assignment is passed out. Individual volunteers are asked to read parts of the syllabus out loud, including the point section of each unit. Teaching Team responds to questions asked by students after each section is reviewed.
Reflection Time: 5 minutes Inquiry Community	Still in the inquiry community, ask students if there are any questions about the syllabus and the grading system. Ask the students the following questions: 1. Have you ever done a research project where you got to choose the topic? If so, how did you feel about it? 2. How are you feeling right now? Do you feel overwhelmed, excited, nervous, etc.?
Notes:	The next workshop will continue to open the project introducing the information search process and peer review. Study buddies will be assigned during the session. The folders with the students' names and some identification of the class should be handed out. Students are expected to have their folders with them every day, and they may be kept in a basket in the library. All materials are to be kept in the folder, and the folders will be assessed at the end of the project.

| Common Core Standards: | RI.9–10.2. Determine a central idea of a text and analyze its development over the course of the text, including how it emerges and is shaped and refined by specific details; provide an objective summary of the text.

RI.9–10.10. By the end of grade 9, read and comprehend literary nonfiction in the grade 9–10 text complexity band proficiently, with scaffolding as needed at the high end of the range.

SL.9–10.1. Initiate and participate effectively in a range of collaborative discussions (one-on-one, in groups, and teacher led) with diverse partners on grade 9–10 topics, texts, and issues, building on others' ideas and expressing their own clearly and persuasively.

• Propel conversations by posing and responding to questions that relate the current discussion to broader themes or larger ideas; actively incorporate others into the discussion; and clarify, verify, or challenge ideas and conclusions. |
|---|---|

Workshop 1

Student Handout: The Assignment, a.k.a. the Syllabus (SAMPLE)

1. **Preliminaries for Research:** Preparations will begin the first week and run through the first several days of research class. You do not have to definitely choose your topic yet, but you should start thinking about possible topics. It is during this time that you will be looking for general information about a possible topic.

   Class time will also be used to prepare for your research.

   Among the topics we will discuss are:
   * *Getting Organized*
   * *The World of Information*
   * *Browsing & Digital Databases*
   * *Going from Big to Small*

   Descriptive Essay "How I Learn"   **10 points**

2. **Begin Topic Research**

   Begin Individual Research

   1st Instrument   **20 points**

3. **Proposal**   **5 points**

   Your proposal is in the form of two double-spaced paragraphs. In the proposal you are persuading your teacher that this is a worthy topic of research and that you will have enough resources to successfully complete and present your topic. The proposal will highlight the following: in paragraph one, an explanation of the topic and where you plan to find the information. Paragraph two will contain any audiovisual aids, realia, and primary source(s) you plan to use, and the form of your presentation such as accompanying dance, costume, graphics, and/or audio. Please include any rough sketches of planned visual aids (posters, objects, costumes, etc.) after the two paragraphs. An example of a proposal will be provided.

4. **Actual Research:** You must provide to the librarian samples of:
   a. **Three (3) Types of Sources**   **10 points**
      Must include:
      * At least one (1) Primary Source
      * At least one (1) Realia
      * At least three (3) other sources, **only one of which may be a specialized encyclopedia—topic specific not general (Wikipedia cannot be used) and only two**

may be approved online sources (website, database, podcast, etc.). One source should be a print source.

- You may certainly use more than five sources including interviews, photography, artwork, etc. Please check with the librarians for appropriate sources.

b. **2nd Instrument**   **20 points**

c. **Research Notes:** 40–45 note cards (we will supply blank cards) about **your subject. Your collection of research notes should reflect more than one perspective and at least five sources on your subject. In other words, we encourage you to find different perspectives of (conflicting or controversial) information about your subject. You will be graded on the quality of your notes.**

   30 of the Research Notes Due   **25 points**

d. **Organizing Your Notes into an Outline**

e. **Backdoor Research & Making Final Notes**

f. **Final Research Notes Due**

5. Presentation Notes   **10 points**

A set of notes on 5x8 note cards that you will use to organize your thoughts and give your speech during the actual presentation. These are not the same as your research notes. You will receive an example in a workshop on presentation notes prior to the due date.

6. Audio/Visual Aids   **5 points**

A poster, audio, prop, or costume must be used. **No video or computer-delivered visual may be used due to time constraints.**

Audiovisual aids make the most important and interesting information in your presentation clear to your audience. Graded on **quality, effort, and relevance.**

NO EXCEPTIONS—*anything submitted for use after this date is not eligible for use in your presentation! Do not show up on presentation day with something new.*

7. Bibliography   **10 points**

A listing of all sources *handled*, even if not directly used in the final presentation. Please note the bibliography will be completed in class using EasyBib.

8. Presentation   **10 points**

The culmination of your research work. Your oral presentation will be a five-minute speech delivered to all of your peers. This will be graded on degree of *interest, organization, content,* and *performance*. **Absences on presentation day are not an option. A letter will go home informing parents/guardians of these important dates. Conflict? See us *AS SOON AS POSSIBLE.***

   3rd Instrument   **10 points**

9. **Reflection**   **5 points**

You will write an in-class reflection essay titled "What I Learned About Myself During This Research." No notes or sources may be used. Extra credit may be given and will be determined by honesty and detailed examples.

10. **Total Effort**   **20 points**

Teachers will determine how wisely and efficiently class time is used and how enthusiastically research is carried out.   **(10 Points per quarter)**

A TIMELINE IS ATTACHED WITH DUE DATES FOR THIS PROJECT

Source to Consult: *MLA Handbook for Writers of Research Papers*—Sixth Edition
http://easybib.com

Evaluation: Your Research and Writing Project grade will be based upon the points described in the syllabus.

Grading: Your final Research and Writing Project grade for the semester will be composed of 160 Points Maximum.

Third Quarter Grade: **80 points (Maximum)**
Fourth Quarter Grade: **80 Points (Maximum)**

Grading Policies:

One semester-long grade will be tallied for this project. That grade will be determined by points earned with the maximum number earned being 160 points. Points are given for the following:

Assignment Graded	Maximum Points Allowed
First Instrument	20 points
Essay	10 points
Proposal	5 points
Sources Due	10 points
Research Notes	25 points
Effort	10 points
First Quarter	80 points
Second Instrument	20 points
Bibliography	10 points
Audio/Visual	5 points
Presentation Notes	10 points
Your Presentation	10 points
Third Instrument	10 points
Essay	5 points
Effort	10 points
Second Quarter	80 points

Assignment Timeline

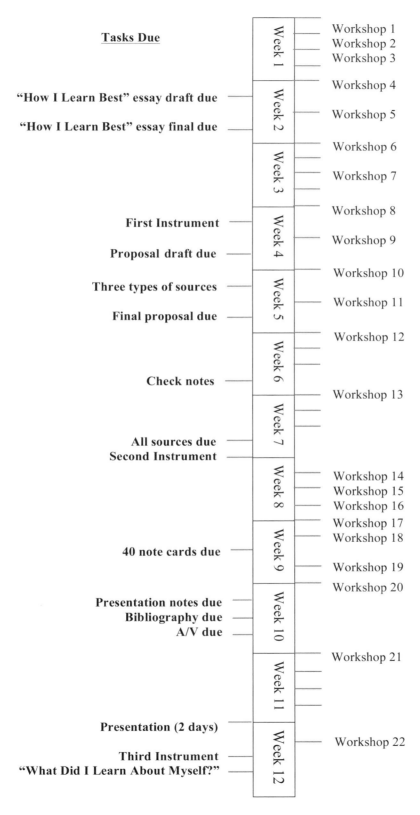

Tasks Due

	Week 1 — Workshop 1, Workshop 2, Workshop 3
"How I Learn Best" essay draft due	Week 2 — Workshop 4, Workshop 5
"How I Learn Best" essay final due	
	Week 3 — Workshop 6, Workshop 7
First Instrument	Week 4 — Workshop 8, Workshop 9
Proposal draft due	
Three types of sources	Week 5 — Workshop 10, Workshop 11
Final proposal due	
	Week 6 — Workshop 12
Check notes	Workshop 13
All sources due	Week 7
Second Instrument	
	Week 8 — Workshop 14, Workshop 15, Workshop 16
	Week 9 — Workshop 17, Workshop 18, Workshop 19
40 note cards due	
	Workshop 20
Presentation notes due	Week 10
Bibliography due	
A/V due	
	Week 11 — Workshop 21
Presentation (2 days)	Week 12 — Workshop 22
Third Instrument	
"What Did I Learn About Myself?"	

Workshop 2

Overview: What Is the Information Search Process and What Is Peer Review?

Almost 30 years ago, groundbreaking research was published about how high school students go about completing a research project and paper. That research which was updated in *Seeking Meaning* (Kuhlthau, 2004) was completed in New Jersey by a former high school librarian. She described the pattern of searching for, finding, and using information for a research paper as the "Information Search Process"—the ISP.

Her research findings (Kuhlthau, 2004) were tested by other researchers on groups of non–high school subjects. The ISP held as a pattern for adult researchers as well. The interesting feature of the ISP is that researchers show a pattern of how they feel while undertaking different stages of research, from the initiation of the project through selection of a topic, exploration of general information, and formulation of the direction of the research to collection of the needed materials to the presentation of the findings. In addition, researchers also show a pattern of thoughts and actions that correspond to the different stages of the research process.

The goal of this workshop is to review the seven stages of the ISP and to provide students with an understanding that three forms of experience accompany each stage: 1) feelings about the project, 2) thoughts about the information, and 3) activities undertaken while handling the information.

Again, an important secondary goal is for the teachers and librarians to reassure the student that the ISP will be conducted as a guided inquiry. The student will develop an individual inquiry to research. The teachers and librarians will be the guides along the ISP journey.

In Handout #2 for Workshop 2 is a section titled "Reflecting on Helping Each Other." Five questions are listed to direct the reflective class discussion. While these questions are not exclusive to the discussion, they reflect typical responses of students who are just beginning to assist and critique their peers. Some students sincerely do not know why they must become involved with peer review. An appeal to the student's patience and trust is important at this point. Eventually, students will understand the significance of the workshop.

Workshop 2: What Is the Information Search Process and What Is Peer Review?

Learning Goals: The goal of this workshop is to introduce the concepts of the information search process and peer review protocol.
Location: Library
Team: Teacher, Librarian, and Resource Guide
Inquiry Unit: This workshop establishes norms and processes for the research project, including individual researcher roles and roles as peer reviewers.
Total Time: 50 minutes

Starter Time: 20 minutes Inquiry Community	On the whiteboard or with an overhead projector the librarian shows the ISP chart and explains the seven stages and three forms of experience. Ask students to remember the last time a research project was assigned. What did they do, how did they feel, and what did they think? Explain the role of the peer review.
Worktime Time: 20 minutes Inquiry Community	The whole class participates in a discussion of what is a study buddy and what is a peer reviewer.
Reflection Time: 15 minutes Inquiry Community	Reflect on helping each other. The class discusses why it is important to help each other.
Notes:	Questions during the reflection may include: A. What can I contribute to my peers? B. What is important about multiple perspectives or different points of view? C. How can I be friendly and critical at the same time? D. Why can't the teachers just help us? E. Why can't I just do the work myself?
Common Core Standards:	SL.9–10.1. Initiate and participate effectively in a range of collaborative discussions (one-on-one, in groups, and teacher led) with diverse partners on grade 9–10 topics, texts, and issues, building on others' ideas and expressing their own clearly and persuasively. 　• Propel conversations by posing and responding to questions that relate the current discussion to broader themes or larger ideas; actively incorporate others into the discussion; and clarify, verify, or challenge ideas and conclusions. 　• Respond thoughtfully to diverse perspectives, summarize points of agreement and disagreement, and, when warranted, qualify or justify their own views and understanding and make new connections in light of the evidence and reasoning presented.

Workshop 2

Student Handout #1: What Is the Information Search Process (ISP)?

Model of the Information Search Process (ISP)

Model of the Information Search Process (ISP)						
	Initiation	Selection	Exploration	Formulation	Collection	Presentation	Assessment
Feelings (Affective)	Uncertainty	Optimism	Confusion Frustration	Clarity	Sense of direction/ confidence	Satisfaction or disappointment	Sense of accomplishment
Thoughts (Cognitive)	Vague ⟶ Focused				Increased interest		Increased self-awareness
Actions (Physical)	Seeking relevant information		Exploring		Seeking pertinent information	Documenting	

Kuhlthau (2004, p. 82)

There are seven stages of the Information Search Process (Kuhlthau, Maniotes, & Caspari, 2007) from initiation through assessment. Three forms of experience accompany each stage: 1) feelings about the project, 2) thoughts about the information, and 3) activities undertaken while researching information.

Workshop 2

Student Handout #2: Introducing the Concepts of Peer Review and Study Buddy

I.   Peer Scholarship

In the land of scholarship, a peer in scholarship is considered a scholarly equal, someone who through his/her own education and practice has a similar knowledge base and similar experiences doing research. Therefore, a peer should be able to assist the researcher in the process of research by providing feedback in the form of constructive criticism and helpful guidance from one scholar to another. For this project, a peer for each scholar will be called a "study buddy" and will be selected by the teacher and assigned early in the project to help the student with tasks such as topic selection, proposal formulation, and creation of presentation notes. The study buddy will be expected to provide peer review and may even be graded for the quality of peer review at different times during the research process. You and your study buddy will also meet with another pair of study buddies to form an inquiry group (something like a study group) to discuss your research and help each other to progress toward your individual presentations.

II. Peer Review

   Q: *Who is my study buddy?*

   A: Your study buddy is someone in your class assigned to you by your teacher who will be your peer reviewer.

   Q: *What does he/she do?*

   A: Your study buddy will be your partner. He or she will not do your research work for you but will give you suggestions and judge (in a gentle, constructive, positive manner) the quality and quantity of your work, such as your research note cards. Your study buddy will time your speech and evaluate your presentation for such qualities as volume, tone of voice, speed of speaking, eye contact, and body language. Your study buddy may also help you figure out your primary source, your realia, and your audio/visual aid, such as a costume.

   Q: *Why do I need him/her?*

   A: You need a researcher-friend, someone who will help you a little and listen to your speech a lot. You need someone who understands what you are going through—each study buddy is a fellow student who is going through the same research process.

   Q: *What are my responsibilities as a study buddy?*

   A: Your responsibilities as a study buddy are to be kind, helpful, and honest, and to remember that research is not easy for most people.

   Q: *What are my responsibilities as a peer reviewer?*

   A: Your responsibilities as a peer reviewer are the same as a study buddy's responsibilities. You are supporting a fellow researcher.

Q: *What is an inquiry group?*

A: In this research and writing project, occasionally teachers will ask two or three sets of study buddies to form a small group together. We will call this small group an inquiry group. The inquiry group broadens the feedback that each researcher will receive from one peer to three or more peers, thus increasing the constructive assistance each researcher will receive.

III. Reflecting on Helping Each Other

Toward the end of the workshop, the teacher may ask the entire class or the inquiry groups to discuss why it is important to help each other during research. The questions involved in this discussion may be:

A. What can I contribute to my peers?
B. What is important about multiple perspectives or different points of view?
C. How can I be friendly and critical at the same time?
D. Why can't the teachers just help us?
E. Why can't I just do the work myself?

Workshop 3

Overview: Understanding Perspective and Bias in Information Sources

The goal of this workshop is for the student to understand the concepts of "perspective" and "bias" as they are encountered in the world of information. For a new high school student, the fact that information encountered might be taken from a distinct, already established viewpoint or might be filtered and understood by employing specific, embedded values, challenges the more naïve belief in the inherent objectivity of a person encountering new information. For the naïve information seeker, information is what it is; the seeker may be changed by the new information, but the seeker will never "change" the information while the information is being encountered.

Thus, to introduce and explain how to understand perspective, one must explain a point of view and how that point of view might alter the "wholeness" of the information encountered. The student handout provides an example from recent history of new information and how perspective might affect the student's encounter.

The concept of bias is fraught with such emotion that a fun example will be used in the workshop to ensure that the discussion does not become an argument. Bias is defined in the handout as "a preference or inclination, especially one that inhibits impartial judgment" (*American Heritage Dictionary of the English Language*, 2011, p. 175). Students are reminded that biases often are grounded not in experience, but in unexamined values. The fun bias employed here is observing how a typical or familiar teacher usually appears and what happens to the viewer when that appearance changes.

In both examples of perspective and bias the student is encouraged to think of the particular response experience, to extrapolate from that personal experience some picture of how anyone either presenting or receiving information can "get in the way" or alter the objectivity of the information by simply being there.

Workshop 3: Understanding Perspective and Bias

Learning Goals: The goal of this workshop is to introduce students to the concept of informational perspective, and to demonstrate the effects of unconscious bias.
Location: Library
Team: Teacher, Librarian, and Resource Guide
Inquiry Unit: This workshop bridges the gap between brainstorming research ideas and developing an informed perspective on a research topic.
Total Time: 50 minutes

Starter Time: 15 minutes Inquiry Community	A) Teaching Team stands in front of students dressed in regular teaching attire to talk about where information comes from (6 senses) and how it is delivered (pie chart of 20+ options). Distribute Handout #1 after the pie chart is made on the board. B) Teaching Team shows recent publications of current event: video, print, cartoon, etc.
Worktime Time: Discussion A: 10 minutes Inquiry Community Discussion B: 10 minutes Inquiry Community	Students discuss how they get their information and what kinds of formats of information they prefer. Students are asked to write and then share what they know about the current information event that has been introduced, and how they know it. Teacher defines and discusses definition of perspective and bias.
Reflective Exercise Time: 15 minutes Inquiry Community	Teaching Team asks students to write down 3 descriptive phrases about the teachers. Team is called out, returns two minutes later in "crazy" outfits and wigs or hats with deadpan faces. Teacher asks students to write 3 more descriptive phrases about the Teaching Team. Comparisons are made with before and after descriptions. Students reflect on their biases of teachers' appearances. Distribute Handout #2 after reflections.
Notes:	The emphasis here is on a fun activity to diminish the possibility of negative response to the concept of bias and to emphasize how perspective can change and biases can be challenged with new information.

Common Core Standards:	RI.9–10.2. Determine a central idea of a text and analyze its development over the course of the text, including how it emerges and is shaped and refined by specific details; provide an objective summary of the text.
	W.9–10.3. Write narratives to develop real or imagined experiences or events using effective technique, well-chosen details, and well-structured event sequences.
	• Engage and orient the reader by setting out a problem, situation, or observation, establishing one or multiple point(s) of view, and introducing a narrator and/or characters; create a smooth progression of experiences or events.
	• Use precise words and phrases, telling details, and sensory language to convey a vivid picture of the experiences, events, setting, and/or characters.

Workshop 3

Student Handout #1: Understanding Perspective and Bias in Information Sources (Part I)

We are going to examine four aspects of information today:
1. How do we receive information?
2. How is information delivered to the world?
3. How does perspective affect information?
4. What are informational biases?

1. How do we get information?

Seeing, hearing, tasting, smelling, touching, (and the disputed sixth sense, intuition).

Students are each asked which two ways they best receive information. Most say "seeing and hearing," but are coaxed into considering how the other senses also play into receiving information.

2. How is information delivered?

Students' responses are drawn into a pie chart of sorts.

Some responses were:

- Mail
- Phone/cell phone
- Books
- Internet
- Social networks
- iPod/iPad
- Conversation
- Experts
- Teachers
- Library
- Documents
- Pictures
- Art

- Charts
- Maps
- Search engines
- Encyclopedia
- Lectures
- Social
- Television
- Environment
- Weather
- Performances
- Sporting events
- Concert

Workshop 3

Student Handout #2: Understanding Perspective and Bias in Information Sources (Part II)

3. Perspective and information bias

The Teaching Team is gathered in front of the room. Students are asked to describe the group of teachers (but cannot use general words like: teacher, people, women, etc.). The students must use two or three descriptive words or adjectives. (Descriptions are written on the board)

Magazines featuring some current event such as Occupy Wall Street are presented. Students are asked to write down:

    a. Did you watch any programs about the impact of the event (Occupy Wall Street)?

    b. What did you watch? Did you find it informative—Why?

    c. What was your main source of (Occupy Wall Street) information?

    d. Do you think the (government's response) or (Occupy Wall Street's actions) were responsible? Why/Why not?

    e. Why do you think the event happened (Occupy Wall Street is targeting the 1%)?

(*Note to teachers: Use a widely known current event issue that the majority of students will have read about or been informed of one way or another, enabling them to have formed an opinion.*)

After these questions, the Teaching Team is summoned away for a "discussion." Silly or outlandish costumes are donned in secret. Teaching Team returns to the classroom poker faced and continues the lesson.

Discussion continues with discussion of "perspective" and "bias."

- **Perspective** is defined as: a mental view or outlook . . . an understanding of how aspects of a subject relate to each other and to the whole . . . the ability to perceive things in their actual interrelations or comparative importance (*American Heritage Dictionary of the English Language*, 2011, p. 1318).

- **Bias** is defined as: a preference or inclination, especially one that inhibits impartial judgment . . . an unfair act or policy stemming from prejudice (*American Heritage Dictionary of the English Language*, 2011, p. 175).

Students are asked their responses to (Occupy Wall Street) questions.

Students are also asked to describe how they perceive their teachers now, with the costumes, by writing three descriptive words/phrases on a card. After that, answers should be put in a new column on the board.

- How did a simple change in appearance alter how the students perceived their teachers?

These questions lead into a discussion of how we all have our own perspectives and biases. How/why do perspectives and/or biases form?

Why is this discussion relevant and important to the research/writing project? Some responses students/teachers may give include:

- It is important to get different perspectives.
- When researching, one must be open to different perspectives and try to understand the source's bias.
- When you compare and contrast information from different sources and perspectives about a certain subject, you are doing your own actual thinking, which then leads to your own original ideas about the subject.
- Creative thinking is taking borrowed information from different sources, perspectives, and/or biases and critically thinking about it by comparing, contrasting and then adding one's own ideas or meanings. One of the goals of this project is the development of creative and critical thinking.

Workshop 4

Overview: What Are Learning Styles?

Over the past seven years or so, I've worked closely with Mrs. Schmidt on many guided research projects at GSB. Overall I found several aspects of the guided inquiry process to be extremely helpful teaching and learning tools but, as an English teacher, what I found to be the most interesting for both students and teachers is the identification of learning styles. This practice is not only useful in helping students to identify research topics of interest and how to proceed with their respective research, it is also extraordinarily helpful to the instructor when guiding the student with their topic selection, research, and, more importantly, for gaining an overall understanding of how to help each student thrive and succeed in any curricular or co-curricular environment.

—Laura Wengel, English Teacher, Gill St. Bernard's School, May 2012

In this workshop the student is preparing to use note cards to write a descriptive essay that will describe the student's learning style. The student first has to understand what a learning style is and that a learning style (or sometimes a combination of more than one learning style) might best describe how the student takes information and gains knowledge from the information.

The revolutionary work of educational psychologist Howard Gardner of Harvard University described the concept of a multiplicity of learning styles in the 1993 book, *Frames of Mind*. Since that time, Gardner and other scholars have further researched and defined learning styles, which are now considered, with some variations, to be:

1) Kinesthetic—body smart—use of body and body movement to learn
2) Linguistic—word smart—use of language and reading of words to learn
3) Logical—mathematical/numbers smart—use of number and numerical sequencing to learn
4) Interpersonal—people smart—use of communication and interaction with others to learn
5) Intrapersonal—myself smart—use of self-reflection and self-understanding to learn
6) Spatial—picture smart—use of two- or three-dimensional pictures or images to learn
7) Musical—music smart—use of rhythm and other musical elements to learn

A person's learning style may influence the types and formats of information chosen for research. For example, if a student could choose between three different live performances on a given day, the linguistic learner might choose a dramatic play, the musical learner might choose a musical play on Broadway, and a kinesthetic learner might choose a World Cup soccer game or a performance of the New York City Ballet.

Such choices may also be reflected in the decisions a student makes about a possible inquiry to be researched. A visual/spatial learner might choose to research a photographer. An interpersonal learner might choose to research the nature of comedy.

Therefore, students are introduced to the concept of learning styles to begin preparations for choosing the individual inquiry. Each student will compose a short, half-page handwritten statement in class of no more than three paragraphs introducing the student and describing the student's learning style(s). Highlight three examples of when the student utilized the style and what was learned, then write a brief conclusion.

The goal of the workshop is to understand the concept of a learning style and choose the style(s) that best describe(s) the individual student. Have the student make a list of three examples of when the learning style was employed in: 1) an extracurricular or free time activity not related to "schooling," 2) a favorite class in school this year, and 3) during a recent period of stress, for example, end of term exams, argument with parents, or a competition.

A reflection could take place at the end of the workshop, if time permits, to discuss with the study buddy the different learning styles chosen and the fellow students' perceptions of each individual's learning style.

Workshop 4: What Are Learning Styles?

Learning Goals: The goal of this workshop is to introduce the concept of learning styles, to then choose a style or styles that best describes the student. Students will identify their own learning styles to begin preparations for the research process.

Location: Library

Team: Teacher, Librarian, and Resource Guide (Learning Specialist if available)

Inquiry Unit: This workshop begins the students' identification and understanding of their individual learning styles to help tailor their research.

Total Time: 50 minutes

Starter Time: 15–20 minutes Inquiry Community	Teacher will provide Handout #1 describing Howard Gardner's list of learning styles, and the handout will be read aloud by the students. After the reading the teacher will ask students to volunteer what they think their learning styles might be.
Worktime Time: 25–30 minutes Inquiry Community	Teacher will distribute a sheet of scrap paper and a sheet of lined paper to each student who will use the scrap paper to list three different examples of learning something and how it was learned. The students will attach one of the learning styles to each example. The students will use the second handout and the lined paper to fashion a three-paragraph statement of his/her learning styles, using what they have already formulated. The first paragraph will introduce the student, the second will describe the three examples of learning, and the third will be a conclusion of what the student has identified as his own style.
Notes:	The short statement the students write will not be graded but will serve as an introductory exercise to the descriptive essay. The student has now begun a journey of self-discovery as a budding scholar.
Common Core Standards:	W.9–10.2. Write informative/explanatory texts to examine and convey complex ideas, concepts, and information clearly and accurately through the effective selection, organization, and analysis of content. • Provide a concluding statement or section that follows from and supports the argument presented. Anchor Standard 10. Write routinely over extended time frames (time for research, reflection, and revision) and shorter time frames (a single sitting or a day or two) for a range of tasks, purposes, and audiences.

Workshop 4

Student Handout: What Are Learning Styles?

Learning Styles, according to the respected educational psychologist Howard Gardner (1993), are different ways in which people take in information and learn best. A person can have more than one learning style.

The learning styles description below is adapted from "Gardner's Multiple Intelligences" at http://www.tecweb.org/styles/gardner.html. Permission granted by Carla Lane, EdD and The Education Coalition.

Visual-Spatial—Students with a strong sense of visual-spatial intelligence think in 3-D. Learning tools include "models, graphics, charts, photographs, drawings, 3-D modeling, video, video conferencing, television, multimedia, texts with pictures/charts/graphs."

Bodily-Kinesthetic—Students with a strong sense of bodily-kinesthetic intelligence are very aware of their bodies and their motion and learn "through physical activity, hands-on learning, acting out, and role playing. Tools include equipment and real objects."

Musical—Students with a strong sense of musical intelligence are "sensitive to rhythm and sound. They love music, but they are also sensitive to sounds in their environments." They may turn "lessons into lyrics, speak rhythmically, tap out time." Learning "tools include musical instruments, music, radio, stereo, CD-ROM, multimedia."

Interpersonal—Students with a strong sense of interpersonal intelligence learn by "interacting with others." "They have many friends, empathy for others, street smarts. They can be taught through group activities, seminars, dialogues. Tools include the telephone, audio conferencing, time and attention from the instructor, video conferencing, writing, computer conferencing, e-mail."

Intrapersonal—Students with a strong sense of intrapersonal intelligence understand themselves very well and may "shy away from others." They learn "through independent study and introspection. Tools include books, creative materials, diaries, privacy and time."

Linguistic—Students with a strong sense of linguistic intelligence are masters of words. They learn through "reading, playing word games, making up poetry or stories." Learning "tools include computers, games, multimedia, books, tape recorders, and lectures."

Logical-Mathematical—Students with a strong sense of logical-mathematical intelligence "think conceptually and abstractly, and are able to see and explore patterns and relationships." They learn "through logic games, investigations, [and] mysteries."

Workshop 5

Overview: Descriptive Essay of Your Learning Style

The goal of this workshop is for the student to understand what a descriptive essay is and how one can be written. Description is a method of identifying an object, place, person, event, action, or idea. In the world of information and research, description is one of the best methods of both enlarging as well as specifying or bringing into focus or attention the object, place, person, event, action, or idea.

For example, say that a person with red hair is being described. If one were to describe the person as being a teenage female of average height, that might include a larger number of red-headed girls than if one were to describe the redhead as being 6'4" tall. Both are descriptions that aid in identifying the girl—the first is a broader description; the second narrows the identification of the teenage girl.

As all of these lessons lead to preparing for the presentation of the research, a description whether sparse or extensive adds to the interest of the audience. Students are to be reminded here that their presentations to their peers are virtually spoken into a vacuum. The peer audience may know little or nothing about the topic being presented, so the members of the audience cannot conjure up distinct mental images unless the speaker describes the topic in a lively, imaginative way. Description allows the reader of written work or the listener of the presentation to better understand and grasp the information the student has found in the research. Descriptions can be said to personalize information or to universalize information in both cases, to better facilitate communication and the flow of ideas.

The student should be reminded of the previous lesson on perspective and bias in which students were asked to describe the teachers twice, once in ordinary, everyday teacher wear, and then in extraordinary costumes that challenged the teacher stereotype and removed conventional teacher bias.

Inquiry Group questions might include:

1. Which descriptions were more interesting, fun, colorful, particular and, well . . . more descriptive?
2. Why, what made the description better?
3. How can you describe something without using a string of adjectives?
4. If you compare two things that are seemingly not alike, are you describing?
5. Do you know what a thesaurus is and how to use it to find more precise words?
6. Thinking back on the teacher descriptions both before and after the costume changes in Workshop 3, which words were more descriptive of the teachers? Why?

Workshop 5: Descriptive Essay of Your Learning Style

Learning Goals: The goal of this workshop is to understand the nature of a descriptive essay and to write a brief five-paragraph descriptive essay on a personal learning style.

Location: Library

Team: Teacher, Librarian, and Resource Guide

Inquiry Unit: This workshop begins the formal writing process, and formulates a connection between the writing process and the information search process.

Total Time: 50 minutes

Starter Time: 15 minutes Inquiry Community	Students are handed 5 index cards (4x6) and are asked to hold them aside to make notes, which will then become the basis of a descriptive essay. Students are then asked to volunteer examples with descriptive words of their favorite extracurricular activity and what and how they learned some aspects of that activity. Students may be further prompted by examples the Teaching Team provides. After students write and share several examples, they are asked to describe their favorite class, including what they learned in that class and how they learned it. Finally, several students will be encouraged to share what and how they learned something while preparing for a test or in a time of stress. Handout #1 is distributed. Students are instructed to also use the handout about Learning Styles from Workshop 4.
Worktime Time: 25 minutes Individual Student	Now students are asked to fill out a description on each card about learning: 1) in an extracurricular activity, 2) favorite class, and 3) a time of stress; one card for each category (extracurricular, favorite class, time of stress). After these three cards are filled out, the students will write one card naming and describing himself and his learning style. And finally they will write one card telling the reader what the student intends to research and how it fits into his learning style.
Reflection Time: 10 minutes Study Buddy	The student then "turns-and-talks" to his/her study buddy about the information on his/her cards and then the study buddy, after actively listening, will verbally evaluate the partner's description. Roles are then reversed.
Notes:	Another unstructured workshop can be devoted to actually typing up the descriptive essay directly from the note cards using Handout #1 and allowing the study buddy to proofread the essay before it is turned in.

Common Core Standards:	Anchor Standard 4. Produce clear and coherent writing in which the development, organization, and style are appropriate to task, purpose, and audience.
	W.9–10.2. Write informative/explanatory texts to examine and convey complex ideas, concepts, and information clearly and accurately through the effective selection, organization, and analysis of content.
	• Develop the topic with well-chosen, relevant, and sufficient facts, extended definitions, concrete details, quotations, or other information and examples appropriate to the audience's knowledge of the topic.
	W.9–10.5. Develop and strengthen writing as needed by planning, revising, editing, rewriting, or trying a new approach, focusing on addressing what is most significant for a specific purpose and audience.
	W.9–10.7. Conduct short as well as more sustained research projects to answer a question (including a self-generated question) or solve a problem; narrow or broaden the inquiry when appropriate; synthesize multiple sources on the subject, demonstrating understanding of the subject under investigation.

Workshop 5

Student Handout: Descriptive Essay—"How I Learn Best"

You will write an essay, using note cards, that describes *How I Learn Best.*

You will be able to write a short essay describing your learning style(s).
1) Take one blank note card and answer these three questions after reading the previous handout, "What Are Learning Styles?"

- What is my name and what is my "passion"?
- How do I learn best?
- What kinds of things do I like to learn about? And why?

For example, answering question #1:

"My name is Randi Schmidt and I am passionate about books. I learn best by reading. I take in information visually. In my free time, I enjoy romance novels and time-travel books such as Octavia Butler's book *Kindred.* I especially enjoy reading magazines like *Ode* and *Mother Earth News* that have pictures and text about important social and ecological issues."

Remember a **DESCRIPTION:**

1) Paints a picture
2) Gives an impression
3) Leaves a sense
4) Provides an understanding
5) Gives an illustration

Tips to writing a description:
- Incorporate your five senses to generate sensory details for your essay.
- Try to create a clear and thorough picture for your readers with your words.
- Choose words that help you to construct that picture.

Describe your individual learning style, including the topics and types of things you enjoy learning about. Be as SPECIFIC as you can!

2) Take three blank note cards. While answering the next three questions, use specific examples to illustrate each of your answers on a separate note card. The three specific examples should be taken from real-life experiences.

Three questions for scenarios of real-life learning are:

1. In your free time or in extracurricular activities, name one thing you learned about and how you learned it.

2. In your favorite course at school, name one thing you learned about and how you learned it.

3. While you were studying for midterms or during a time of stress, name one thing you learned about and how you learned it.

Write one card for what and how you learned in each question/scenario.

After filling out the three cards:

3) For the descriptive essay, use the three cards with examples to write three short paragraphs answering each of the questions—one answer per card, one paragraph per card. Use examples that illustrate specifics and have descriptive words within each answer.

Next,

4) On the fourth note card, write a brief introductory paragraph naming yourself, describing yourself, and declaring your learning style(s). Add the three paragraphs that you have done in Step 2 and 3.

5) On the last notecard, add a final paragraph that tells the reader what topic you are thinking about researching, using your learning style(s).

You are now done with the draft of your descriptive essay. And you completed the essay using three cards of notes about your learning style during free time, in your favorite class, and during a stressful time. You also used information from an introductory note card and finally a note card indicating what you intend to research based upon a description of how you learn.

Research in the Selection Stage of the Information Search Process

Workshop 6: Browsing and Searching
Workshop 7: Going from Big to Small
Workshop 8: Information Sources
Workshop 9: Proposal—What Topic Have You Chosen?

During the Selection Stage, four workshops are scheduled and detailed herein. This is the time when students are digging more deeply into the research materials because soon, a research topic must be proposed. Interlibrary loans are initiated as students survey possibilities for obtaining sources to be named in their proposals. At least three or more unstructured workshop times should be scheduled for students to brainstorm a possible topic, and to explore sources and ideas. Teacher and librarian should circulate among students to offer individualized attention. The librarian should also be available to discuss interlibrary loans.

   During selection, students will become more optimistic as a topic comes into view and the project becomes personalized.

Workshop 6

Overview: Browsing and Searching

Research (Rice, McCreadie, & Chang, 2001) has shown that humans spend some of their information handling time (i.e., their time searching for something) in the act of browsing, including browsing to find out information, which is called *preparatory browsing*. Browsing can be defined as an information-seeking behavior that "allows people to enter an information space with little in the way of . . . labels for their need and to navigate to information that may be helpful" (Allen, 1996, p. 163). When a person browses, he/she gets a bigger picture by looking around and seeing what is available before a choice is made. The metaphor of shopping may be used to describe browsing; the student goes shopping in the library or online in the same way he/she might shop for a pair of shoes, especially a pair of shoes he/she wants but is not sure where they are located. At the mall the student goes from one shoe store to the next, looking in the windows, going into the stores, seeing the available shoes, maybe trying shoes on, getting the prices, and then comparing and contrasting the shoes that he/she likes and that fit. All of this browsing may actually take more time than one would expect, to find the one pair of shoes to eventually buy. The search for anything, whether shoes or information, takes time. So the student should take that time and actively browse.

Several types of browsing are encouraged in the library. Examples of non-database or non-Google types of browsing include:

1) Walking around and looking at the different sections of the library to see where the reference books are, where the stacks of regular books that one can take out are, what kinds of maps and videos the library has, where the current print newspapers are kept.

2) Walking through the book stacks and seeing what kinds of architecture or photography or any other subject books the library has, what kinds of art books are available, if the library has a biography the student might need, what kinds of cookbooks are on the shelves, how many sports car books the library has.

3) Looking through the online catalogue for other sources of information about a topic.

4) Talking to a librarian or a teacher to discuss other sources of information about a topic.

5) Further browsing might include sitting down with a reference book and reading about a possible topic to choose.

The student should begin this browsing experience with the understanding that the research journey has just begun and the path ahead is not yet marked clearly—**and that is alright!** The student has plenty of time.

One outcome of browsing for a topic is exposure to basic information about a possible topic. For browsing, one lightly reads or even skims possible sources and may encounter new terms or words that refer to or better describe the possible topic the student is considering. Such exposure to newer words, terms, or descriptions allows the student researcher to use previously unknown search terms when searching for information on the databases. New terms therefore can both expand and/or focus the student's access to information.

Teachers should note that students are often uncertain why browsing is a productive activity, and why they cannot just jump in and begin collecting their required number of sources to get it done quickly. Students may need to be reminded that because they know so little about their possible topics of inquiry, browsing and learning a little something before the heavy-duty research begins may improve the possibility of more in-depth research. Background browsing will eventually produce a better search for the topic material, introducing the student to basic information and better search terms for later in the research.

Workshop worktime is, more or less, unstructured time during this research project. Students know the tasks to be completed and are expected to work at those tasks. However, some students may not have the self-discipline, experience, or will to do so unassisted. Other students may have learning styles that are initially challenged by the seemingly unstructured "free time," especially inside a substantial library space where the student is supposed to be browsing. It is entirely possible that one or more students may have never seriously browsed in a library before—although that is hard to believe!

The students, as an inquiry community, can be reminded of three time restrictions or caveats to this assignment:

1. The browsing time in class will be supervised by the teachers and librarians who will step in to intervene, if it appears the time is being wasted.

2. Only two structured workshop periods are allotted for browsing, and the result of that time should be shown in possible topic choices and location of possible source information. Otherwise, the student will have to spend time outside of class such as a free period with the librarians supervising his/her browsing.

3. An effort grade is given to each student as part of the course evaluation. Displays of the student's effort begin with the browsing sessions within the library or on digital resources.

The librarian and teacher, as they circulate during the worktime, will be able to pick out those students who may need models of the adults browsing or who may need one-on-one attention and directions during the workshop as they browse.

Workshop 6: Browsing and Searching

Learning Goals: The goal of this workshop is to begin exploring resources in the library and digital collections.

Location: Library (with access to computers)

Team: Teacher, Librarian, and Resource Guide

Inquiry Unit: In this workshop, students will become familiar with digital and print resources within the library and database collections. These resources will be used to build and support the student's own perspective and idea for a research project. Additionally, support may be provided to students by the librarian or teacher in individual or small-group interviews about research interests and goals.

Total Time: Two 50-minute periods.

Starter Time: 15 minutes Inquiry Community	With the Handout #1 the librarian explains what browsing is and why it is important. Start with a fantasy scenario with parents handing the student $200 to spend at the mall. The student will have to figure out how he/she is going to spend it. The Teaching Team sets up the analogy of shopping at the mall to have the students think about how they will use their funds to make the most of the possible resources (goods) and discusses the meaning of the metaphor and what browsing in a library means, in the stacks, databases, and reliable internet sources.
Worktime Time: 35 minutes Inquiry Community	Distribute Handout #2. With the librarian operating a projector, the students are asked to identify and reference the online catalogue within the library and choose one topic they are interested in (this may or may not be directly related to their final topic). This begins a demonstration of the catalogue search. The librarian operating the projector will facilitate as students find three different sources that address this topic on their own computers. The students will first search by subject, and then by the name of a known author. They can also search by the title of a particular work that interests them. If they have time they can enter an advanced search where they can use two subjects. Students will make notes on findings, titles, authors, and Dewey call numbers. When they have a Dewey library call number they should find the work in the stacks and explore nearby books on similar subjects.
35 minutes Study Buddy	Distribute Handout #3. This is an introduction for some and a reintroduction for others of researching a database (online information collection). Students will be directed to a list of the three databases used during this period. Study buddies will work together. Each database will be explored, using a similar protocol to the Dewey search, and students must find one magazine or newspaper article about a possible subject choice.

Reflection Time: 15 minutes Study Buddy	Students will have conversations with their study buddies about what they found, what was interesting, what they did not find, and what possible topics they might explore.
Notes:	Having identified the students' learning styles, examined perspective and bias, and explored some of the resources available, the student will think more constructively about a possible topic that will fit into interests and experiences. The next workshop will narrow down the topic to a more manageable size. At the Teaching Team's discretion, one or more extra unstructured workshops may be used for students to further browse and evaluate material on possible subjects.
Common Core Standards:	RI.9–10.6. Determine an author's point of view or purpose in a text and analyze how an author uses rhetoric to advance that point of view or purpose. W.9–10.7. Conduct short as well as more sustained research projects to answer a question (including a self-generated question) or solve a problem; narrow or broaden the inquiry when appropriate; synthesize multiple sources on the subject, demonstrating understanding of the subject under investigation. W.9–10.8. Gather relevant information from multiple, authoritative print and digital sources, using advanced searches effectively; assess the usefulness of each source in answering the research question; integrate information into the text selectively to maintain the flow of ideas, avoiding plagiarism and following a standard format for citation.

Workshop 6

Student Handout #1: Browsing Lesson

This is a lesson about how to start looking for something. We will begin with a fantasy. . . . Imagine that your parents hand you $200 and tell you to spend it.

Explain browsing using the example of a visit to a mall that you are not familiar with:

1. Why do you go to the mall?
   - Shopping
   - Food
   - Sales
   - Friends
   - Movies
2. What would you do once you got into the mall?
   - Check that you still have money!
   - Ask someone where you are.
   - Find out where you are.
   - Look around.
   - Look at map/directory.
   - Go to the food court.
   - Go into different stores.
   - Browse by comparing products and prices to try to figure out what to buy.
   - Look at displays/window shop.
   - Get ideas.
   - Cover a wide area and several shops at the mall.
3. Why is the shopping mall a metaphor for browsing for information?
   - Common activity especially with information.
   - Large portion of early information seeking activity.
4. Why should you browse the online public access catalog (OPAC)?
   - See OPAC handout.
5. What kind of in-library browsing for information is possible?
   - OPAC
   - Stacks (the print book collection)
   - Reference area (encyclopedias, atlases, guides, handbooks)
   - Audio/Visual area (films, tapes, photo packs)
   - Librarians
   - Teachers
   - Database collections of cataloged information online

Workshop 6

Student Handout #2: Searching Tips for the Online Catalogue of Library Holdings (SAMPLE)

The Online Catalogue of the High School Library Collection

Quick Search: Enter word(s) or names:
> SEARCH = broad keyword search (all indexes)
> AUTHOR / TITLE / SUBJECT = index-specific searches

EXAMPLE: Type in Hemingway, Ernest or Ernest Hemingway

Clicking on	Search	will find all items that have "Ernest Hemingway" anywhere in the catalog
Clicking on	Author	will only find items that list "Ernest Hemingway" as the author
Clicking on	Title	will only find items that have "Ernest Hemingway" as a part of the title
Clicking on	Subject	will only find items that treat "Ernest Hemingway" as the topic/subject (literary criticism/biographies)

Advanced Search
- allows use of Boolean terms—AND, NOT, OR—to broaden or limit search
- allows choice from a broader array of indexes

Boolean Terms:
OR—expands search possibilities (DNA OR genetic code) OR is more!
AND/NOT—limits search possibilities (Civil War AND Confederacy NOT Union).
The more words used with AND and NOT, the more specific the search becomes.

Indexes:
Pull down the list of choices; make sure choice corresponds to search terms entered.
- Series Index:
  Choose a series such as "Opposing Viewpoints" or "Reference Shelf."
- Call # Index:
  Type in "973.2" to get American History or "398.2" for Folktales/Fairy Tales.

More searching tips:
- Adding a period "." at the end of a word will pull up only exact matches for that word. Typing "genes" brings up only entries with the term "genes".
- An asterisk "*" after the word will allow for various endings of a term.

Typing "gene*" will search for gene, genes, genetic, genetics, genetically, etc., to broaden your search.

When you find an item you like and want to know what else is physically adjacent to it on the library shelf, use the ⎵Look Right⎵ and ⎵Look Left⎵ buttons that appear in the item's catalog entry to browse.

FOR ELECTRONIC RESOURCES HELD BY THE LIBRARY:

As eBooks become more popular, library catalogues are incorporating them into their collection listings. The eBook will appear as a link in those library catalogues.

Electronic databases subscribed to by libraries will not necessarily be accessed through the catalogue but will be listed on the library or school Web page as a database.

Workshop 6

Student Handout #3: Electronic Databases—Digital Searching

A database is an online collection of mostly full-text current or historic newspapers, magazines, scholarly journals, books, and so on that are located on the website of the database publishing company, which gathers and creates that collection of information.

For example, the company Proquest collects many newspapers such as the *New York Times* and publishes those papers on its database. E-Library, another database, has some different information resources than Proquest. On E-Library a researcher can find transcripts of public radio programs in the database. Dozens, even hundreds, of databases exist for research purposes. This library subscribes to twelve major databases. All databases that we subscribe to can be accessed in the library and should not require passwords. We will give you a handout with all the database information to allow access. This information is also available on the school's website. Subscription databases, which our library purchases each year, allow remote access from places other than our school, with some requiring specific passwords.

The database information handout provides names of all databases available for this library, along with user information and passwords.

NOTE WELL:

An article pertinent to your topic from one of the databases usually is an acceptable source of information because it has been previously edited and published, thus establishing some authority for the information.

In general, with the Research and Writing Project, you are encouraged to use materials from databases rather than simple websites to find your information. *In fact, you may not use a general website without librarian permission.*

Workshop 7

Overview: Going from Big to Small

This project has been very challenging for me from the beginning. Although there was no shortage of information to be found on chocolate, it was difficult sorting through that information and finding the facts I needed to create an amazing presentation. I eventually decided to settle on presenting the history of chocolate. From there it was fairly easy to write the 40 note cards, a task which seemed daunting at first.
            —Max Lieblich, Student, Gill St. Bernard's School, December, 2010

Research is an activity in which, ultimately, the researcher makes order out of chaos. When a student begins to look up information for a topic, of which the student has little prior knowledge, chaos often reigns. The student may print a few articles, order some books, check out a video from the library, and find a long entry in a specialized encyclopedia. At the beginning of the search, the student is empty handed; and then all of a sudden, the student has several items—perhaps even too much information.

Before all this information can be digested the student should stop, sit down, and think about what the topic is. In high school research, because students have little background or historical perspective, topics chosen are often too big. Typical student choices may be:

World War II	President Kennedy
The Sixties	Ice Cream
Fashion	Muhammad Ali
Soccer	Audrey Hepburn
The Movies	The Circus

Any of these general topics are just too big. But for the young researchers, such big topics might be quite interesting.

The goal of this workshop is to begin the process of taking a topic that is too big and impossible to adequately represent in a five-minute presentation and to make a choice of a smaller topic (a subtopic) within the same category of information. To narrow or shrink the topic so that the student may produce an interesting five-minute presentation is what this workshop is all about.

At first the student should choose an article, film, photograph, or one specific information structure and "consume" it. Read, look at, view, listen, or think about it. What does that piece of information say about the chosen topic? Ask questions of the piece of information. Is it interesting? Does it lead to other questions? What are the questions? Does one part of the topic seem more interesting or does everything not seem interesting? Perhaps the student should find another piece of information on the broad topic and repeat the questions. If the student cannot maintain high interest in a broad topic, another information source should be "consumed." If one part of the topic seems more interesting, the student should point his research in that direction.

For example, a student chooses to study "The Sixties" and soon finds references in one or two sources to "protest music," which seems very interesting. Protest music becomes the direction of the student's research. If, however, the student says he wants to change his topic at this point, he should be allowed to change, and the topic choice begins anew.

Workshop 7: Going from Big to Small

Learning Goals: While this workshop is intended as a lesson about going from "bigger" topics to "smaller" topics, it is really a lesson on getting more specific. This is where the researching part of the ISP process truly begins.
Location: Library (with access to computers)
Team: Teacher, Librarian, and Resource Guide
Inquiry Unit: In this workshop, the student narrows his topic by interacting with specific informational texts and more defined information about a possible topic.
Total Time: 50 minutes

Starter Time: 20 minutes Inquiry Community	Teacher distributes and students read aloud Handout #1. Ask the students to list things they are thinking about researching on the board. Then the Teaching Team will have the students look again at the programs from previous years and ask the students to discuss the specificity of the presentation titles. The teacher may point out an example: "This student began with the topic *The Sixties*; the title is now *Political Unrest in the Sixties*. How is this different? What are some other titles that may have come out of that original topic?" The teacher shows a few clips of the presentations from previous years to illustrate the specificity and focus of smaller topics.
Worktime Time: 25 minutes Inquiry Community	Teacher distributes Handout #2. Students and the Teaching Team will spend this time looking at an online catalogue, looking at a specialized encyclopedia, and resources suggested by the librarian. Additionally, students who have advanced more rapidly could begin to explore the resources. Using the example of attending a party, the student is asked how she decides where she is going to go, who she is going to look for, and so on. The importance of the arbitrariness of the first information search actions become apparent because the students will, more often than not, end up somewhere different from where they started. The emphasis is that often where we end up is different than where we expected when we began the research. Anything that triggers a focus of interest is welcomed at this point in the project.
Reflection Time: 5 minutes Study Buddy	Students will sit with study buddies and discuss how they are narrowing down their topics. The students will get feedback from the study buddy. Guiding questions will be on the board: 1. What is your general interest in the topic? 2. Within that general interest, what have you found specifically so far? 3. What kinds of sources have you looked at? 4. Are they good sources? (See Handout #2 Section B for requirements for good information.)
Notes:	The next workshop will familiarize the students with different kinds of information sources to complete the exploration stage.

Common Core Standards:	RI.9–10.6. Determine an author's point of view or purpose in a text and analyze how an author uses rhetoric to advance that point of view or purpose. W.9–10.7. Conduct short as well as more sustained research projects to answer a question (including a self-generated question) or solve a problem; narrow or broaden the inquiry when appropriate; synthesize multiple sources on the subject, demonstrating understanding of the subject under investigation. W.9–10.8. Gather relevant information from multiple authoritative print and digital sources, using advanced searches effectively; assess the usefulness of each source in answering the research question; integrate information into the text selectively to maintain the flow of ideas, avoiding plagiarism and following a standard format for citation.

Notes:	This exercise demonstrates how individual perceptions, etc. can affect the information presented and why primary sources are so important for in-depth research.
	The librarian can also use this opportunity to mention constructivist learning theory, and that information builds on itself—sometimes well, sometimes not so well—which is why good-quality sources are important.
	Perspective, bias, and other factors affect how someone receives information. Brainstorming is not something students are used to. It is important for the student to experience the collaboration of brainstorming and see how it can move an idea forward. This prepares students for the task of identifying their topics. It is helpful to emphasize the importance of everything the teachers and students are doing. By the conclusion of the workshop a student should be actively thinking of a topic. At the discretion of the Teaching Team, another unstructured workshop can be devoted to further exploration of the topics and/or individual student conferencing.
Common Core Standards:	W.9–10.2. Write informative/explanatory texts to examine and convey complex ideas, concepts, and information clearly and accurately through the effective selection, organization, and analysis of content. • Introduce a topic; organize complex ideas, concepts, and information to make important connections and distinctions; include formatting (e.g., headings), graphics (e.g., figures, tables), and multimedia when useful to aiding comprehension.
	W.9–10.8. Gather relevant information from multiple authoritative print and digital sources, using advanced searches effectively; assess the usefulness of each source in answering the research question; integrate information into the text selectively to maintain the flow of ideas, avoiding plagiarism and following a standard format for citation.
	SL.9–10.1. Initiate and participate effectively in a range of collaborative discussions (one-on-one, in groups, and teacher led) with diverse partners on grade 9–10 topics, texts, and issues, building on others' ideas and expressing their own clearly and persuasively. • Propel conversations by posing and responding to questions that relate the current discussion to broader themes or larger ideas; actively incorporate others into the discussion; and clarify, verify, or challenge ideas and conclusions.
	SL.9–10.2. Integrate multiple sources of information presented in diverse media or formats (e.g., visually, quantitatively, orally) evaluating the credibility and accuracy of each source.

Workshop 8

Student Handout: Examples of Information Sources

Information Event: A meteor crashes into a soccer field. That is the event. You observe it and call three friends in biology class. A reporter is doing an article on the event. The reporter talks to the people you called.

Who or what is which source? Identify the primary source, the secondary source, and the tertiary source.

Three Types of Information Sources

Information is imperfect. Example: the telephone game. But all information comes from a source. There are three types of information sources:

1) Primary Source: A primary source is information taken directly from a person, event, location, or material at the point of occurrence. The primary source *may not* be totally accurate. The primary source can display a bias and experiences the event from his/her own perspective. For example, you are researching the first landing on the moon. Primary source information from that landing would include statements from the astronaut, the flag he planted, rock he might have picked up, or photos taken during the landing. Primary source information is directly related to the event.

2) Secondary Source: A secondary source is information that a person provides after he or she has gotten the information from a primary source. Secondary source information can be created just after the event or years after the actual event. The secondary source *may not* be totally accurate. A good example of secondary source information about the first landing on the moon would be a story written by a reporter who interviewed the astronaut. Secondary source information is one person removed from someone who actually experiences an event.

3) Tertiary Source: Tertiary source information is information that a person provides after he or she has gotten secondary source information and reinterpreted or retold it. Tertiary source information can also be created years after the event and has no direct contact with the event. Therefore, tertiary source information is two people removed from someone who actually experiences an event. The tertiary source *is often* the least accurate—but not always.

Playing the Source Game: Primary, Secondary, and Tertiary Sources

Three student volunteers are pulled from the classes to represent primary, secondary, and tertiary sources. Another student volunteer is pulled to serve as the "information event" and tells the primary source (once and out of earshot of secondary and tertiary) two nonsensical sentences. One example: "Three pink monkeys type on a yellow chair. I walk on square clouds and a red encyclopedia." Primary source must then report it to the secondary source privately, and then the secondary source must report it to the tertiary source privately. After this, the three sources and information event present individually in front of the class but not in front of each other. Starting with the tertiary source, with the other sources out of the room, each reports what that person heard. It is important to point out that tertiary is two people removed from the information event and that the secondary source is one person removed from the information event. Only the primary source had direct contact with the information event. A recorder will privately record, on a sheet of paper, each source's report. After all are done, the three sources' reports are written on the board to compare.

Teacher explains that the information event itself is not a primary source. Examples could be a weather event, war, a dog doing a funny trick, or a scenario between two freshmen. In this exercise, the speaking of the sentences is the event.

Brainstorming a Primary Source

You can brainstorm primary sources based on individual topics and write them up on the board. You can include interviews, direct quotes, fragment of an official product, and so forth. **Remember that for the project the primary source *must be approved* and may not be an immediate family member.**

Ex: Psychic interview, quote from newspaper article by Red Smith, direct quote from Paul McCartney, Nabisco public relations person.

Examples of Brainstorming Session:

1. As a class, you can brainstorm.

2. Or, you can break up into inquiry groups and continue to brainstorm on each individual's primary source for student research.

Workshop 9

Overview: Proposal—What Topic Have You Chosen?

The preliminary workshops are now over as the student prepares to finalize a proposal for a presentation. The early stages of initiation, selection, and exploration have come to a close as the research proposal is prepared so that it can be scrutinized by the teacher and librarian. The goal of the workshop is the production of a two-paragraph proposal that informs the proposal reader of the topic to be researched and indicates at least three of the five resources to be used for the presentation. As in all scholarly proposals, the researcher is setting out the plan of his/her scholarship, convincing the reader that enough early-stage work has been done to justify the choice of topic and to ensure adequate resources are available to complete the project.

In the case of young scholars, the proposal focuses and narrows the topic to make the research and note taking more manageable and to encourage a concentrated effort. The teachers and librarian guide the student to specific sources that pinpoint, or more definitely specify, the chosen topic based upon already-encountered information from those sources. In other words, the student's proposal should reflect the work the student has already done and should project work the student anticipates doing in the coming weeks. That work will round out a now acquired small body of information.

Introducing a proposal can be simplified by creating a teacher or librarian model inquiry and creating a model proposal document, as has been done on the student handout for this workshop. The sample proposal for the research project is in Handout #1: "Universal Appeal of Chocolate Chip Cookies" is presented in the same two-paragraph format required for the scholars and offers a pattern for students to use in preparing a research proposal.

The two paragraphs hold different information about the research and projected presentation. In the first paragraph, the student indicates the main topic of his research. The student also provides the reader with at least three distinctly different and specific aspects of the inquiry. In the second paragraph, the student explains what type of audio/visual aid will be used, what realia will be incorporated into the presentation, and what primary source of information the student has identified for possible use in the research.

After the two paragraphs have been composed, the student is asked to graphically depict, as simply as possible, the information to be placed in the research poster.

Handout #2 is provided to the students to be filled out and turned in to the teacher. The handout will serve as an organizing record for the teacher/librarian to pull together the presentation proposal and to record preliminary notes and needs prior to the presentation, as well as to be used for assessment of the proposal.

Workshop 9: Proposal—What Topic Have You Chosen?

Learning Goals: The goal of this workshop is for students to produce a two-paragraph proposal of the topic to be researched, including identification of some of the sources that will be used.

Location: Library

Team: Teacher, Librarian, and Resource Guide

Inquiry Unit: This workshop begins the introduction and explanation of the individual student's focused research.

Total Time: 50 minutes

Starter Time: 10 minutes Inquiry Community	Teacher passes around a plate of home-baked chocolate chip cookies with a copy of a model proposal for the research project, "Universal Appeal of Chocolate Chip Cookies." (Teacher distributes Handout #1) Teacher explains that today's workshop will result in a proposal from each student. Students are asked to read the model proposal.
Worktime Time: 25 minutes Inquiry Community	Students gather their already-found resources and write draft proposals, modeled after what has been provided. The Teaching Team circulates to assist students and check resources. Draft proposals are completed.
Reflection Time: 10 minutes Study Buddy	Teacher distributes Handout #2. Two or three volunteers put proposals on the board while study buddies use the handout to check one another's draft proposals and suggest additions or corrections.
Time: 5 minutes Inquiry Community	Entire class reflects on whether the model helped students to write a proposal. They discuss how the study buddy feedback can be used to improve future drafts.
Notes:	The students now have produced a two-paragraph draft proposal. The next workshop time could begin with finalizing the proposal before dipping into more source finding. At this point in the guided inquiry, the Teaching Team should determine whether another unstructured workshop period should be devoted to continuing source finding.

Common Core Standards:	W.9–10.4. Produce clear and coherent writing in which the development, organization, and style are appropriate to task, purpose, and audience.
	W.9–10.5. Develop and strengthen writing as needed by planning, revising, editing, rewriting, or trying a new approach, focusing on addressing what is most significant for a specific purpose and audience.
	W.9–10.8. Gather relevant information from multiple authoritative print and digital sources, using advanced searches effectively; assess the usefulness of each source in answering the research question; integrate information into the text selectively to maintain the flow of ideas, avoiding plagiarism and following a standard format for citation.

Workshop 9

Student Handout #1: How to Write Your Proposal

Proposal: Your proposal is in the form of a two-paragraph, double-spaced paper. In the proposal, you are persuading your teachers that this is a worthy topic of research for your inquiry and that you will have enough resources to successfully complete and present your topic. You must name at least three of your sources. The proposal will highlight the following: in paragraph 1, an explanation of the topic and where you plan to find information; in paragraph 2, indicate any *audio/visual aids* you will use, the *realia*. and *primary source(s)* you plan to use and the form of your presentation. Please read the example proposal below.

Universal Appeal of Chocolate Chip Cookies

For my Research and Writing Project, I plan to investigate the reason for the "universal appeal of the chocolate chip cookie." I plan to look in historical materials including the *New York Times* on the history of baking cookies and using chocolate. I also plan to look at recipe books such as *Cookies: At Home with the Culinary Institute of America* directly dealing with cookies. I will also use one online source that deals with baking and in particular cookie baking, which is titled, "Cookies.org."

For my audio/visual aids I will distribute several copies of chocolate chip cookie recipes and do a photo chart depicting the increased consumption of cookies for the past 50 years. I plan to do a "person on the street interview" asking 50 random students about their personal cookie preference and then chart these results. I will also interview a cookie baker from Coco Luxe Shop for my primary source material. As my realia, I will bring in items used in the making and baking of chocolate chip cookies as well as some very delicious examples of a truly fine cookie.

On My Poster:

A) Cookie Preference Survey Results
B) Photos of the History of Cookie Consumption
   1. Original Toll House Cookie Recipe
   2. Early Bake Sales
   3. Inception of Girl Scout Cookie Sales
   4. Covers of Cookie Recipe Cookbooks

1	2
3	4

Workshop 9

Student Handout #2: What Topic Are You Proposing?

Student Name: Class Period:

Topic: Study Buddy's Name:

Why have you chosen this topic?

Give us two or three good reasons for choosing this topic:

This Handout will be used by your Teaching Team to plan the presentation schedule.

Research in the Exploration Stage of the Information Search Process

Workshop 10: Understanding Responsibility to Intellectual Property
and the Concept of Plagiarism
Workshop 11: How to Take Research Notes

During the Exploration Stage, two workshops are conducted and detailed herein. However, because the students will begin taking notes from sources already found, at least two or more unstructured workshop times should be scheduled between workshop 11 and workshop 12, so that there is additional time to identify and explore possible sources. The students may continue thinking about the proposal topic and turn to the Teaching Team for help. While exploration of the proposal topic may be framed as a research question, the Teaching Team does not require the student's inquiry to be articulated as an actual research question in this project. See the Preface for an explanation of the **inarticulated question**.

In addition, the teacher and librarian should jointly teach the workshop on intellectual property and plagiarism to impart the seriousness and full weight the workshop warrants.

Workshop 10

Overview: Understanding Responsibility to Intellectual Property and the Concept of Plagiarism

As the time approaches for the student to begin taking notes from sources for the research, the concepts of intellectual property and plagiarism must be introduced in the context of borrowing information while undertaking research. The goal of the lesson is to explain student responsibilities to intellectual property and to reinforce the concept of plagiarism as being against the expectations of school and society.

Research can be explained as an act of searching for and processing information that is not already known by the researcher. In order to do the searching and processing, the student goes out to the world—sometimes through the library, sometimes in other directions such as in databases, on the internet, or through multiple means of media and personal connections—to find out what is already known by others about the research topic. Then, finding out what others know, the student must borrow some of that information. The information that is being borrowed from others (unless a direct quote acknowledges the information belonging to a third person) is the intellectual property of the borrowed source (person), which means that the words, idea, design, organization, or image being borrowed comes from the work of the mind of that source. That source could be an author, speaker, artist, performer, architect, dancer, and so on—whoever created the intellectual material being borrowed.

When a student borrows words, ideas, designs, organizations, or images, one of three choices must be made:

1. The student can "lift" the text, idea, design, organization, or image **directly** and transfer it to his own work. If so, the student must indicate in his own work that has happened with quotation marks and specific source citation. Here the student is quoting his/her source or directly copying.

2. The second choice a student can make is to borrow a small amount of intellectual property of the source and paraphrase it, in other words use the source's concept(s) but put the source's concept into the student's own words and then cite the source in text, bibliography, and/or program notes.

3. A third choice a student can make is to take a larger amount of source information, the words, ideas, designs, organization, or image and borrow it by summarizing the information in the student's own words, ideas, designs, organization, or image. But here again, the student must publicly acknowledge the borrowing and summarizing of the source information by citation, bibliography, and/or program notes.

In short, the student faces two imperatives when undertaking research. First, the student must borrow the information to do the research. And second, the student must publicly acknowledge whose intellectual property he borrowed doing the research.

The challenge to the teacher is to emphasize the importance of the student's responsibility to publicly acknowledge the intellectual property of the source and to directly quote, paraphrase, or summarize the material that is borrowed from the intellectual property owner.

Public acknowledgement of intellectual property comes in the form of citations of the borrowed material within written text; a bibliographic entry of the written, recorded, or spoken text; an acknowledgement of quotation; or use of the idea within a speech and program notes for a performance or recording.

A helpful exercise to introduce the concepts of intellectual property and plagiarism is the following:

> When the class first begins, hand each student one small 3x5 note card. Ask the students to define or describe what each believes is meant by the word "plagiarism." Ask the students next to turn the card over and define or describe what is "intellectual property." Chances are a variety of definitions will appear.

Then explain that we, as individuals, each have a responsibility to intellectual property just as we each have a responsibility to physical property.

Responsibility to intellectual property occurs at three different levels of society:

1. Legally with copyright laws and laws against theft.
2. Ethically/morally with the belief that stealing is not right, the Golden Rule requires each person to "do unto others," and so on.
3. Socially with the understanding that society depends upon the transmittal and accountability of information that can be tracked and verified because **new knowledge builds upon older knowledge and new knowledge permits society to solve problems.**

Plagiarism, then, becomes the illegal, immoral, and asocial use of someone else's (the borrowed information source's) intellectual property, which can be:

- **Words**

- **Ideas/Concepts**

- **Designs**

- **Organization**

- **Image**

without public acknowledgment.

Workshop 10: Understanding Responsibility to Intellectual Property and the Concept of Plagiarism

Learning Goals: The goal of this workshop is to explain the student's responsibilities to intellectual properties and reinforce the severity of plagiarism and its negative scholastic, legal, and moral implications.

Location: Library

Team: Teacher, Librarian, and Resource Guide

Inquiry Unit: This workshop initiates student understanding of the hard work that research involves, including finding, evaluating, note taking, and source identification.

Total Time: 50 minutes

Starter Time: 10 minutes Inquiry Community	Teacher hands each student one 3x5 note card and asks each student to define or describe what he/she believes is meant by the word "plagiarism." Turn the card over and define or describe "intellectual property." At the end of this exercise teacher will distribute Handouts #1 and #2.
Worktime Time: 25 minutes Inquiry Community	Teacher solicits student-generated definitions and places them in two columns on the board: 1) plagiarism and 2) intellectual property. Librarian discusses the concept of borrowing information and how one records the borrowed information. The librarian also recaps the three different types of information sources, primary, secondary, and tertiary—all of which may be quoted, paraphrased, or summarized. All sources are defined as someone else's intellectual property.
Reflection Time: 15 minutes Inquiry Groups	Inquiry groups gather to discuss what they think of intellectual property and what kind of intellectual property each participant would like to create in his/her lifetime. This will be shared out, and the Teaching Team will identify that intellectual property belongs to its creator, and if it is used by someone else as their own, this is stolen property.
Notes:	Each student should reflect on how it would feel to learn that someone had taken his/her created intellectual property and not given the student credit for it.

Common Core Standards:	Anchor Standard 10. Write routinely over extended time frames (time for research, reflection, and revision) and shorter time frames (a single sitting or a day or two) for a range of tasks, purposes, and audiences. W.9–10.8. Gather relevant information from multiple authoritative print and digital sources, using advanced searches effectively; assess the usefulness of each source in answering the research question; integrate information into the text selectively to maintain the flow of ideas, avoiding plagiarism and following a standard format for citation. SL.9–10.1. Initiate and participate effectively in a range of collaborative discussions (one-on-one, in groups, and teacher led) with diverse partners on grade 9–10 topics, texts, and issues, building on others' ideas and expressing their own clearly and persuasively.

Workshop 10

Student Handout #1: Understanding Responsibility to Intellectual Property

Research is an act of searching and processing information that you do not already know. When you research, you are admitting that you do not know something and you are going out into the world to find what other people know about the subject. When you do this you are saying that you must borrow information from others. This information that comes from others belongs to others—it is some other person's intellectual property; you are borrowing it.

When you use the borrowed information you may do so in three ways:

1. You may use exactly what someone else has created whether that creation is in words, ideas, design, organization, or image. If you are directly borrowing words, then you must indicate that you are quoting someone. If you are directly borrowing words, ideas, design, organization, or image, you must indicate that it is exactly the borrowed material.

2. You may use someone else's words, design, organization, or image and put that information into your own words, idea, design, organization, or image. An example of this is when you paraphrase a statement that someone makes. You produce in your own words someone else's idea. If you are putting someone else's words, idea, design, organization, or image into another word, design, organization, or image, this is a paraphrase type of borrowed material.

3. You may take a significant number of words, ideas, organization, design, or images from someone else and summarize the meaning or impact of the words, ideas, organization, design, or images. If you do this, you are still borrowing the original words, ideas, organization, design, or images and summarizing them yourself.

When you quote, paraphrase, or summarize material that you have borrowed, you are taking it into your head and there it is connecting with your own ideas and experiences. This gives the borrowed information meaning for you. That meaning begins to create new ideas from the borrowed material. These new ideas are your own ideas but they have a basis in the borrowed material.

As a young student you are just learning how important it is to do research so that you, too, can come up with new ideas. This progress from researching and borrowing material, to making meaning of the borrowed material by mixing it with your own experiences and knowledge thus producing new ideas, is the basis of most human progress. Research is an important means by which the human race betters itself.

Workshop 10

Student Handout #2: The Concept of Plagiarism

What is intellectual property and what responsibility do we have to it?

Intellectual property is the product of someone's thoughts, ideas, and analytical or emotional response to those thoughts or ideas. Our responsibility to intellectual property is:

1. Legal

2. Ethical/Moral

3. Social

What is plagiarism and what responsibility do we have to avoid plagiarism?

Plagiarism is the illegal, immoral, and asocial use of someone else's:

- Words
- Ideas or Concepts
- Design
- Organization
- Image

KNOWLEDGE BUILDS UPON OTHER PRIOR KNOWLEDGE:

IT DOES NOT MATTER WHETHER YOU QUOTE, PARAPHRASE, OR SUMMARIZE INFORMATION AND IT DOES NOT MATTER WHETHER THE INFORMATION IS FROM A PRIMARY, SECONDARY, OR TERTIARY SOURCE. **ALL BORROWED INFORMATION *MUST BE CITED.*** THAT MEANS THAT YOU MUST TELL YOUR READER OR LISTENER OR VIEWER, IN THE CORRECT STYLE INDICATED BY YOUR TEACHER, THAT YOU HAVE BORROWED THIS INFORMATION FROM A SOURCE. THE CITATION TELLS YOUR READER THE NAME OF THE SOURCE AND WHERE YOU FOUND IT. **IF YOU DO NOT DO THIS YOU MAY BE ACCUSED OF STEALING INTELLECTUAL PROPERTY THAT YOU BORROWED, WHICH IS CALLED PLAGIARISM. PLAGIARISM IS AN OFFENSE ACADEMIC INSTITUTIONS ON ALL LEVELS TAKE *VERY* SERIOUSLY.**

The information in this lesson is a necessary prelude to the Note Taking Lesson.

Discussion of the meaning of and responsibility to borrowed information, and holding oneself accountable for that borrowed information, will follow in the inquiry groups.

Workshop 11

Overview: How to Take Research Notes

As the class continued, I was angry when we were assigned 50 note cards. On first impression this seemed unnecessary. We were not ever going to use all of those note cards during the five minute presentation. Why did we have to make so many? This did not make sense until later in the seminar class. But anger was one of the feelings of the seminar emotional roller coaster.
— Harald Parker, Student, Gill St. Bernard's School, December, 2010

Research note taking can be explained as a convenient and neat way to keep track of information found and borrowed to be used later in the student's presentation. If each student had a photographic memory, the research note card might not be necessary as the researcher could, from memory, find the borrowed information to be used.

However, if a student would like to keep track of the found words, ideas, designs, organizations, or images about the research topic, a note card is a fairly easy way to hold the information. And, if the note card is not too big the student will not have to write excessive notes on each card. In fact, teachers should recommend **only one idea** on each note card of between two and four sentences. Thus, the required 40–45 note cards would hold perhaps 130 total sentences, about what is needed for a five-minute presentation of research.

Rather than jumping right into note taking of the research topic, students should practice making at least one of each of the three types of note cards—1) the quote note, 2) the paraphrased note, and 3) the summarized note—together as a class. The Student Handouts titled "Research Note-Taking Activities" suggest three separate activities—one for each type of note.

Each student should be reminded again of the individual's responsibilities to the intellectual property that will be borrowed when note taking actually begins and the borrowed information goes onto the note card. Each student assumes a legal, ethical, and social responsibility to report accurately by quoting, paraphrasing, and/or citing the borrowed information for future use.

Remind each student to keep track of the research notes and keep them in a place where the notes will not get lost! The research folder, which is kept in the library, is a safe place.

No lesson in the research process for students is fraught with more negativity and teenage angst than the lesson on research note taking. Students often do not enjoy note taking and wish they did not have to learn note-taking skills. Why do this? What is the purpose and why can't a student just cut and paste? Thus, teaching research note taking is often not an easy task.

The student is first introduced to a direct quotation note. Break the class into study buddy groups and ask each student to place the study buddy's last name in the upper left hand corner of the card, indicating the author of the book. The student is then asked to leave the upper right hand corner of the card blank (for future use) and to place in the middle of the card a two-sentence direct quote note (with quotation marks). The direct quote is taken from the imagined book that the study buddy has written. In the lesson on note taking and throughout the research project, students are constantly reminded that each note card should only contain one idea because when it comes time to organize notes for a presentation, one-idea note cards are easier to organize.

Students are told that with the exception of an occasional one-sentence direct quote note, most note cards will contain two to four sentences about the same idea.

After the student writes a two-sentence direct quote note from the study buddy's book, the student must then place the title of the book (or a first word abbreviation of the title) and the page number of the book where the direct quote is found, in the bottom right hand corner of the note card. Students then share examples of the quotes and the book titles with their fellow students by placing them on the whiteboard in card format.

Now comes the difficult part of the lesson, as the student learns how to compose a paraphrased note. Until this part of the lesson, students enjoy thinking of titles for their study-buddy's books and then have fun thinking of content to fashion into a direct quote of two sentences. But now the hard thinking is required.

First, the study buddy pair must exchange the note cards containing the direct quote note. Now each student is holding a note card with a direct quote from the imaginary book he/she has written. His/her last name is on the upper left hand corner of the direct quote card as the author of the quote. He/she is now expected to paraphrase the direct quote.

Taking another blank note card, the student is asked to reword the direct quote note for both sentences. The reworded note should have the same essential meaning as the direct quote but contain altogether different words. The only words that may be reused from the direct quote are proper nouns or names of things. Reactions to this task begin almost immediately when the students start to write. Furrowed brows give way to whispers and raised hands, informing the teacher that this is hard, words cannot be formed, and asking why the task must be done. Gently but firmly, the teacher coaxes and urges the students onward.

After the students have completed paraphrasing, students are asked to go up to the board and copy the paraphrased note under the existing direct quote note still on the board, written by the study buddy. The ensuing discussion touches upon the need to not simply rearrange the same words for a paraphrase. Using examples of the students' own paraphrased notes, the teacher points out that sometimes the paraphrased note is richer and more descriptive or interesting than the original direct quote note. The class learns that a paraphrased note contains information of a few words to a few sentences and, generally, conveys one to four sentences of information.

At this time, in spite of much moaning and head shaking, a begrudging acceptance descends upon the class and students can now turn with the teacher to create the third type of research note, the summary note. The teacher explains that a summary note, like a paraphrased note, is written to sum up, again in the student's own words, but contains a larger chunk of information than just a few words, a few sentences, or a paragraph. A summary note encapsulates a brief coverage of several paragraphs, pages, or even a chapter. Here again, the student must write a summary note in his own words.

Each student is now given one more note card and is asked to write a summary note about the lesson just learned in today's class. Finally, the student is asked to read the newly composed summary note so that the class may critique it. The teenage angst has disappeared and laughter often accompanies the summary note readings and critiques.

Workshop 11: How to Take Research Notes

Learning Goals: In this workshop the student is introduced to, and practices, three types of note taking for use of borrowed information: 1) quote, 2) paraphrase, and 3) summary note.

Location: Library

Team: Teacher, Librarian, and Resource Guide

Inquiry Unit: In this workshop the student learns to make notes from borrowed information, so he can use this skill in transferring received information into his own written note cards.

Total Time: 50 minutes

Starter Time: 10 minutes Inquiry Community	Librarian and teacher bring in one favorite short quote each and write it on the board. After the quotes are on the board, student volunteers are called upon to paraphrase each quote. Five 4x6 note cards are handed out to each student. Librarian distributes Handouts #1 and #2.
Worktime Time: 25 minutes Study Buddy	Students are broken up into study buddy pairs. Using the note cards, each study buddy first gives a two-sentence quote that is from his/her own imaginary book. Using the teacher's model, the student will then place the author's name (study buddy's name) on the upper left hand corner. The student will put the name of the made-up study buddy's book and the page number of the quote on the bottom right hand corner. The card is complete. Then the students switch roles. After each has created a direct quote note, then each must use that quote note to paraphrase the quote (put the quote into his/her own words).
Inquiry Community	Examples of student-generated direct quote notes and subsequent paraphrase notes will then go on the board. Inquiry community discusses how difficult it is to paraphrase and how important it is not to cheat by plagiarizing. The whole community is asked to make a summary note of two to three sentences about what happened in the workshop session.
Reflection Time: 15 minutes Inquiry Community	Students should be informed that this workshop marks the beginning of taking research notes of all borrowed material. They should be told that they are expected to make *at least* 40 note cards during the course of their research project. Only 10 percent of them should be quote notes. They will probably make more note cards than they use because weaker or less important notes will be edited (weeded) out. Students will have three weeks to make research (borrowed information) notes. One helpful way to keep track of sources used in the note cards is by color coding the sources, either using a different color note card for each different source or by using different color highlighters to indicate on the card each different source. Students reflect as a community on the act of note taking.

Notes:	Each note card should contain only *one* idea of two to four sentences in length. This is very important for the subsequent "Organizing Note Cards" lesson.
Common Core Standards:	SL.9–10.1. Initiate and participate effectively in a range of collaborative discussions (one-on-one, in groups, and teacher led) with diverse partners on grade 9–10 topics, texts, and issues, building on others' ideas and expressing their own clearly and persuasively. • Come to discussions prepared, having read and researched material under study; explicitly draw on that preparation by referring to evidence from texts and other research on the topic or issue to stimulate a thoughtful, well-reasoned exchange of ideas. W.9–10.8. Gather relevant information from multiple authoritative print and digital sources, using advanced searches effectively; assess the usefulness of each source in answering the research question; integrate information into the text selectively to maintain the flow of ideas, avoiding plagiarism and following a standard format for citation.

Workshop 11

Student Handout #1: How to Take Research Notes

The students first repeat after the teacher, "When I do research, I am doing research because I do not know a lot about _____. I am going out into the world . . . to borrow info."

How do you "hold" information?

– record it

– photograph it/picture it

– take notes

Notes are made from borrowed information.
There are three types of notes:

1. Direct quote: copying a textual note verbatim or exactly word for word from a source.

2. Paraphrase: taking an exact statement from someone and putting it into your own words. This is usually one sentence to one paragraph.

3. Summary: a large amount of information taken from someone else that you can boil down or condense to a short note in your own words. Usually the borrowed information is more than one paragraph to several pages.

Using a direct quote example for a book, the students are shown how to properly cite a source on a note card.

Author's Last Name   (**Absolutely Leave Space Blank**)

Notecard Format

- The note itself goes here.
- Record **one idea** per notecard.
- "Quotes" if quoted, must have quotation marks around the info.
- Ten percent of all the notecards may be quote notes.
- Full sentences must be used in note cards.
- Avoid bullet points if possible on your note cards.

*Source Title or Source #
Page # of Information!

---

*Rather than continuously renaming your source on the notecard you may instead number or color code your source.

Workshop 11

Student Handout #2: Research Note-Taking Activities (Part I)

Direct Quote Note Activity:

Pair up with your study buddy. Without showing each other, make up an imaginary book written by your study buddy. On the note card, write the author's (buddy's) last name, the title of the book, the page number, as well as a direct quote from his/her book (with quotation marks). You "make up" your study buddy's quote. Then take turns sharing your direct quotes with the rest of the class, making sure to include all of the necessary information. On the back of this card and all future note cards you make, you should write the question that this quotation, paraphrase, or summary note answers. **You should have no more than 10 percent of your notes be direct quotes.**

Paraphrase Note Activity:

The term "paraphrase" is explained.

Again, work with your study buddy. In this activity, you invent another title of your own book and invent a quote or use the previously invented quote. Your buddy writes down your quote and bibliographic information on a note card. Then, your buddy must paraphrase the quote that you created on a second notecard. Switch roles and repeat the process. The cards are shared aloud with the class. It is important to stress that when you paraphrase, you cannot use any of the same words unless the words are proper nouns that are in the direct quote. Also, *notes on cards must be in complete sentences*.

Summary Note Activity:

The term "summary" is explained.

You must now summarize the entire lesson in a few sentences. You must be sure to include all pertinent bibliographical information.

Example:

```
Schmidt (teacher who is the author of
the lesson)

Summary Note in 2–4 full sentence(s)

                        Class Name (Period 4)
                                        Date
```

Remember: Notes can be made from texts, interviews, observations, programs, class lectures, pictures, movies, music, and conversations. **You are still borrowing material in all of these circumstances.**

In total, 40–45 note cards should be made, possibly more than you need. You will probably not use all of your note cards for your presentation because you will edit out the weaker, unnecessary information before writing your presentation notes. You may also color code your sources or the note cards to keep yourself organized.

Workshop 11

Student Handout #3: Research Note-Taking Activities (Part II)

1. Direct quote note: Copy the *exact words* from sentences you wish to use. Put quotation marks around them "like this." **Only quote one idea per notecard**. Can be two to four sentences.

2. Paraphrased note: Rewrite sentence(s) using your own words. Only use and paraphrase one idea per notecard. Use full sentences. Can be two to four sentences.

3. Summarized note: Take several sentences or paragraphs and summarize in your own words. Use full sentences. Can be two to four sentences.

Research in the Formulation Stage of the Information Search Process

Workshop 12: What Are Realia and Why Use Them?
Workshop 13: Using and Making Notes from a Primary Source

During the Formulation Stage, two workshops are conducted and detailed herein. The "heavy lifting" or real work of finding and noting information about the student topics goes on during the formulation stage. Therefore, the teacher and librarian should plan for three or more unstructured workshop times for note taking, estimating that students can make about five to eight cards per workshop. During these workshops, the Teaching Team constantly circulates and checks note cards to assist students who may need intervention or simply a bit of help. At this stage, the students' focus on the research and interviews or other primary source interactions (which will require additional unstructured work time) begins and extends into the collection stage.

Workshop 12

Overview: What Are Realia and Why Use Them?

As the student is finishing the research note cards and interacting with a primary source, preparations begin in earnest for the final presentations. One special and fun feature incorporated into the presentation is the use of realia, which provide a three-dimensional aspect to the research topic.

Students generally have not encountered the term "realia," which can be described as objects directly related to the research topic. Realia is something that really belongs to the topic, it is not a prop that represents the topic; therefore realia do not stand in or substitute for the topic.

Realia are part of the topic. One good example to distinguish a prop for a presentation from realia for a presentation comes from a student researching Ben and Jerry's Ice Cream. A prop could be a dish of plastic scoops of ice cream. Realia for that student would be two gallons of Ben and Jerry's ice cream that sit on a table with two scoopers and dishes during the five-minute presentation, right before a scheduled break in the afternoon program. If you think students will pay attention to that realia, you are correct.

The teacher, while describing to the class what realia are, can then produce several different objects and ask the students to imagine research topics for each article of realia.

Using the model presentation of "The World's Best Chocolate Chip Cookies," the realia of a large plate of homemade chocolate chip cookies is presented to the class and consumed as inquiry groups get together to discuss possible realia for each student's project.

The use of realia, whether they be hand-held objects, musical instruments, food, costumes, textiles, tools, or animals, adds a personalized, often sensory dimension to a student's presentation, bringing to life the student's information search process and setting the stage for more involvement by the audience.

Such involvement is immediate. When food, animals, or performance with instruments, equipment, or tools are presented, such presentations may also require another venue apart from an ordinary stage, which further adds to audience involvement. A research presentation on chocolate requires a visit to the student café to sample hot chocolate realia, whereas a student presentation on hippotherapy requires a visit outside to listen to the presentation with a hippotherapy horse beside the presenter.

We have presided over hundreds of presentations throughout the years with as many as 80 five-minute presentations spread out over two days. We understand that keeping the students' attention as they listen to their peers becomes paramount. Realia with occasional corresponding changes in venue aid in keeping the student audience involved.

Workshop 12: What Are Realia and Why Use Them?

Learning Goals: The goal of this workshop is to introduce the concept of "Realia" and its importance in the research-gathering process.

Location: Library

Team: Teacher, Librarian, and Resource Guide

Inquiry Unit: This workshop introduces "Realia" (a three-dimensional direct connection to the students' research topics.) It also explains the real-world significance of topics.

Total Time: 50 minutes

Starter Time: 15 minutes Inquiry Community	Librarian will bring in homemade chocolate chip cookies for students to eat and contemplate as realia. Teacher will bring in several diverse items, for example, an apple, a wooden statue, a dog bowl, and a flower. Teacher will give students a definition of realia and explain its place in a research presentation. Teacher will distribute the handout and ask students to give examples of possible topics for the realia items. For instance, the apple could be realia for projects on pie-making, gravity, or William Tell.
Worktime Time: 20 minutes Inquiry Groups	Break students into study buddy pairs or inquiry groups to discuss possible realia for their individual topics. Students should keep notes on possible realia.
Reflection Time: 15 minutes Inquiry Community	Whole class comes together to discuss potential realia for proposal topics.
Notes:	Study buddy and inquiry groups helping each other with realia gathering has been shown to provide a bonding experience. One student, last year, was studying Henry Ford. His study buddy's father had a Model T, which he lent for realia (the actual car was transported to school as part of the presentation). The students are now good friends.
Common Core Standards:	Anchor Standard 1. Prepare for and participate effectively in a range of conversations and collaborations with diverse partners, building on others' ideas and expressing their own clearly and persuasively. Anchor Standard 5. Make strategic use of digital media and visual displays of data to express information and enhance understanding of presentations.

Workshop 12

Student Handout: What Are Realia and Why Use Them?

Realia are tangible items that are directly related to a specific topic. Realia are real. They represent the reality of the idea, concept, theory, person, or event that you are researching. When you observe and handle realia, you are learning something about your research topic. The dictionary says that realia are "real things . . . objects such as coins, household items or natural specimens . . . drawn from real life . . . used in classroom instruction" (*American Heritage Dictionary of the English Language*, 2011, p. 1464).

Museums are filled with realia. Your own house is filled with realia. Your room is filled with teenage realia.

In research, realia bring your topic to life and make it more observable. For example, if you are researching an unusual soccer play, the realia of soccer balls used to illustrate the movements on a coach's chart make the soccer play more observable.

Does the realia of an old vinyl recording played on a record player make Elvis Presley's music more real?

Discuss with your study buddy and list on this page possible realia for your topic.

Workshop 13

Overview: Using and Making Notes from a Primary Source

The goal of this workshop is to reintroduce and reinforce the concept and function of a primary source of information, to ensure student understanding of the importance and usefulness of the primary source.

Each student in this project is required to consult at least one primary source of information about the research topic and incorporate notes taken from the primary source into the presentation speech.

True scholarship is dependent upon the research and use of primary source information, which has been defined in Workshop 8. Primary source information takes the scholar/researcher closer in time and space to the actual information event. While primary source information may not be totally accurate and almost always reflects a bias, it is nonetheless an authentic source of information that is provided through an unquestionable direct connection or experience of the information event.

Students sometimes confuse a *primary source* of information with a *main source* of information. They are *not* the same thing. The *main source* of information is that source from which the student got the most research notes. The *main source* does not have to be a primary source. It could be a secondary or less likely (in this assignment) a tertiary source. But the student should be reminded that *primary source* information adds a certain richness or "meatiness" to the subject matter that is difficult to achieve without it. That is not to say that the primary source is easy to obtain nor that the actual primary source can be obtained. In some cases, the student must use a photocopy or facsimile of the primary source. An example of this would be the student who is researching the book *Catcher in the Rye* and the cover of the book. The student might not be able to obtain a primary source, such as a manuscript, or first edition cover of the book. The student, however, could get a facsimile or photocopy of the first edition, pages or cover.

Primary sources can be used in different formats, but regardless of the primary source format, the source provides some information that could be gained by the researcher. Often, a student with a learning style that is neither verbal nor analytical may use sources that are not printed, textual, or data driven.

The student should be informed that a primary source can provide information passively by just being there and offering obvious statements. However, a good, thorough researcher will interrogate (actually question) the primary source to dig into and get broader or deeper information.

To gain the information from such sources, the student must learn to interrogate the information source to optimize what information can be learned from it. Such interrogation techniques as questions, observations, and background references are called for regardless of whether the source is an interview; video clip; photograph; costume; document; map; musical, theatrical, or sports performance; or personal journey.

Two student handouts are provided to assist the student in interrogating the source. By no means should the questions listed be considered complete, although some of the basic questions identifying the source, its location, and its connection to the information are strongly suggested.

The primary source should not necessarily be the initial source. In fact, if the student is conducting an interview with a primary source or viewing photos, video clips, or original artwork for a primary source, it is better for the student to interact with several other sources first to get some background information, which will then raise questions in the student researcher's mind. Those questions can become the basis for the interview or visual artifact being interrogated.

The interview process is the original inquiry tool. The Schmidt Ninth Grade Writing and Research Project requires a primary source. Getting students to truly understand what a primary source is can be difficult. Schmidt's primary, secondary, and tertiary source lesson is invaluable to teach this complex concept. Additionally, with the plethora of materials found on the internet, from YouTube to TED Talks, it is necessary to explain the editing process, the filter, that often transforms what seems to be a primary source, such as an interview, into a secondary source. A great activity to demonstrate the power of the editing process is to have students record each other making a statement and then have them edit it so that the edited statement is contrary to the original statement. This can also be done by taking quotes from a newspaper and having students "edit" them into a counterstatement.

The challenge to having students use edited material is for a student to find a 10- to 30-second UNEDITED clip or portion of the secondary source that can be used as a primary source. I ask students to picture themselves at the site of the recorded event or interview and imagine the following: If you were there, what would you have heard or witnessed live, thus unedited? While mining a secondary source for a primary source nugget is useful, I try to steer the students away from this method of fulfilling their primary source requirement when possible in favor of the interview.

A wonderful life skill to learn is the art of the interview process. Interviewing a subject enables a student to take his/her research to the next level. Students will truly synthesize and understand the information they have researched. First, the student must find and identify an appropriate interview subject. Next, a student must write appropriate interview questions. The interview process takes more initiative and time exerted by the student to actively locate an interview subject and schedule an interview time. As "in person" interviews are preferred, the student may be encouraged to use technology such as "Skyping," "facetime" or video conferencing. If the interview is recorded, a student MUST ask permission to record the interview. When an interview is recorded, the student can truly focus on the content of the interview and not worry about keeping accurate notes until after the interview is completed. E-mail interviews may also be used. The student must remember to either quote the interview responses or paraphrase them when presenting the interview finding. Mrs. Schmidt and I worked together to develop the steps of the interview process as outlined in the Student Handout #1.

I can still remember my first interview. I was in third grade and I interviewed my maternal grandmother. Clara Reusch Keller was born in Ulm, Germany, in 1913. The youngest of four children, her father was murdered in a case of mistaken identity. Young Clara was good at math, but she was not able to continue her education due to lack of funds. At the age of 16 years old, Clara could not find work in the depressed German economy and wanted to move to Switzerland. "Switzerland," my great-grandmother replied. "Why don't you just move to America?"

Almost 30 years later, I can still recount the details of my grandmother's early life. The project for me was the perfect blend of interest in a topic and being able to ask questions, just like the Schmidt Guided Inquiry Project. To my eight-year-old mind, I was the first, the only one to ask these questions and then to receive this information. I now knew something! Knowledge is empowering. As any parent knows, children ask questions, lots of questions. Experts tell us this is how young children figure out how the world works, or so I tell myself after the umpteenth "Why" of my six-year-old son Jack. Asking questions is innate. Interviewing a source is a process.

I honed my interview process at ABC News. As I worked to produce segments for Good Morning America, *I would do my background research and identify experts to interview. From a physicist in Texas, I learned the how and why an accident at 5 a.m. will disrupt traffic for hours after. After the conviction of Libyan terrorists responsible for bombing Pan Am Flight 103, I was honored to interview my former high school vice principal Bert Ammerman, who lost his brother in the crash. After Charles Gibson completed an interview with John Travolta, Mr. Gibson discussed with me his favorite part of the interview. During the interview, Mr. Travolta discussed how exciting and thrilling it was for him when he landed a plane and the disembarking process began. It was the newness, the novelty of the information obtained during the interview, that made this interview with a celebrity different and interesting.*

Timing an interview during the research process is critical. A student must have enough information to find an appropriate interview subject and then to write the interview questions. Students need to be taught the process of the interview question. No yes-or-no and single-word responses, please. As the interview progresses, a student needs to be able to truly listen to the interview subject's answers and to follow up intelligently. I ask my students to listen and to think. Use your instincts. Does an answer need clarification? Ask! Finally, I always have the students not leave the interview until they ask the final question, "Is there anything you would like to add?"
—Amy Mai Tierney, Seminar Teacher, Gill St. Bernard's School, June, 2012

Another point when the primary source can be interrogated is after gaps or holes are found in the research notes. At that time, questions can be addressed to the primary source. The answers may close the information gaps and fill in the holes in the research.

Workshop 13: Using and Making Notes from a Primary Source

Learning Goals: The goal of this workshop is to reintroduce and reinforce the concept and function of a primary source of information from an interview or nontextual material.
Location: Library
Team: Teacher, Librarian, and Resource Guide(s) (Photography or Art Teacher and School's Star Basketball Player)
Inquiry Unit: This workshop is an enjoyable way to introduce and practice skills of interviewing, and interrogating nontextual informational material.
Total Time: 50 minutes

Starter Time: 15 minutes Inquiry Community	Teacher introduces star athlete from the school's basketball team and describes his/her contributions to the team. Students are asked to formulate at least one open-ended question to ask the player. Students are given Handout #1.
Worktime Time: 15 minutes Study Buddy or Inquiry Group	Teacher or student volunteer writes questions and the player's answers are recorded on the board as the questions are asked. Each student makes a note on a note card with one question and its direct quote answer or brief paraphrase. Study buddies or inquiry groups get together and discuss what they learned from the questions. Each group comes up with one or two more questions they would like to ask the player. Basketball player circulates among groups to answer additional questions.
Reflection Time: 10 minutes Inquiry Community	Class gathers together to discuss the interview ideas and compare notes and how one must ask specific questions during an interview.
Notes:	If there are 10 minutes remaining, the photography or art teacher can introduce how the student can interrogate an image to find primary source information and indicate that notes can be taken from that image. Students are given Handout #2. If no time remains, a second workshop can be devoted to art and photography.
Common Core Standards:	W.9–10.2. Write informative/explanatory texts to examine and convey complex ideas, concepts, and information clearly and accurately through the effective selection, organization, and analysis of content. • Use precise language and domain-specific vocabulary to manage the complexity of the topic. RI.9–10.7. Analyze various accounts of a subject told in different mediums (e.g., a person's life story in both print and multimedia), determining which details are emphasized in each account.

Workshop 13

Student Handout #1: Primary Source Information: Interview or Survey (Workshop A)

If you are using an interview or a survey to obtain primary source information, please be aware that preparation and brevity are both necessary to execute a good interview or a good survey. Have all your questions typed up and ready to begin before you start the interview or survey. Put one question on each note card and leave space to write the answer. If possible, please audio-record the interview for accuracy, as then you can truly focus on the content of the interview and not worry about taking notes. If you do audio-record, you must first ask permission from the person you are interviewing.

Guidance for Interview
(In person, by telephone, or via e-mail)

1) **Name, Title, and/or Organization (Identify Source)**
2) **What is your relationship with the topic? (Establish authority of source)**
3) **How long have you been involved with the topic? (Establish authority of source)**
4) Question of your choice—for additional follow-up?
5) Question of your choice—for additional follow-up?
6) Question of your choice—for additional follow-up?
7) Question of your choice—for additional follow-up?
8) Question of your choice—for additional follow-up?
9) Question that clarifies any previous answers, if needed.
10) **Is there anything else the authority (interviewee) wants to add?**

From your ten-question interview you should be able to answer at least some of the following questions: Who did what, when, why, where, how? If you conduct a personal interview, especially with someone you do not know well, it is always good to send a thank-you note.

Guidance for Survey

1) **Your survey should be short—no more than five questions.**
2) **The population that is surveyed should be at least 30 people (for statistical distribution).**
3) **The people surveyed should either represent one group of people—all ninth graders (for example), or be a broad group of people—students, teachers, staff, parents (for example).**
4) **Questions should have yes/no answers, a scale of 1–5 type answers, or some preference choices. You are not looking for complex information or answers.**
5) **You should leave at least one week to execute your survey.**

Both the interview and the survey may be executed in one of three ways: 1) personally, face to face; 2) by telephone/cell phone; or 3) online with an e-mail or online survey format. You must always ask formal permission of the person being interviewed or surveyed before you begin. Your permission request comes in the form of an introduction of yourself as interviewer/ surveyor and an explanation of what you are doing research on (your topic) and why.

Workshop 13

Student Handout #2: Primary Source Information:
Video Clips, Photography, or Artwork (Workshop B)

If you have been unable to obtain primary source materials, three additional possibilities of information are: 1) short clips from longer, edited films or videos that can directly portray accurate "at the moment" information; 2) photographs; and 3) original artwork. For example, an edited video of basketball player Michael Jordan is not considered a primary source. However, within that video may be actual brief footage of him and his marvelous style of play taken during the moment of play. That brief footage can be used as primary source material.

You should view the footage and ask questions of the video clip (interrogate the clip) such as: Where and when was the game? Which team was playing? How did Jordan's style of play look? And what is the clip trying to portray of Michael Jordan the basketball player? Note cards should be made with each of your questions on one card, along with the answer gained from viewing the video clip.

The same technique of questioning can be applied to an original photograph or facsimile taken "at the moment" or an original artwork or facsimile of an original artwork created "at the moment." For example, if you are researching "Bonnie and Clyde," the infamous bandits of the 1930s, and cannot find appropriate primary sources, a copy of the photo of the famous couple shot to death by lawmen in their getaway car can serve as a facsimile of a primary source photograph. You may look at the photo and ask questions about what is pictured. Such questions as; Who is in the photograph? When and where did the event take place? What does the photograph portray about the subjects at the time? Why was the photograph taken? Answers to such questions may be found not only by viewing the photo but also in other texts or in ready reference materials online or in print. Be sure to ask the librarian for help if needed.

For an original artwork, often a blurb or caption under the printed copy of the work gives the title, the artist who created the work, and the year it was created. Databases for artwork or art books may contain more detailed descriptions to aid the student observing the artwork. Again the student interrogates the work asking such questions as; What is the artwork about? Why was this art created? Is there a specific style to the work? What is my response to the visual depiction?

Research in the Collection Stage of the Information Search Process

Workshop 14: Organizing Your Research Notes for an Outline
Workshop 15: Judging Your Research Notes and Looking for Gaps
Workshop 16: How to Do Backdoor Research

During the Collection Stage, three workshops are conducted and detailed herein. At this stage, work must be completed that is thinking intensive and creative. Students must finish their note taking prior to the organization of the research. At least four extra unstructured workshop times should be scheduled to allow students to finish organizing their research notes and decide what gap needs to be filled in the research findings. Completion of this stage may require homework time (unusual for this project) and should be scheduled. The next set of workshops initiates the preparation for the presentation after the collection stage is complete.

Workshop 14

Overview: Organizing Your Research Notes for an Outline

After I had gathered information, putting it into a speech wasn't as hard as I thought it would be. Actually, it was pretty easy with all the organization we did on the note cards. From this I learned how important skills like organization are and how it pays off in the end.

—Emmy Gordon, Student, Gill St. Bernard's School, December, 2010

Part 1

The goal of this lesson is to organize the student's research notes so that an organically produced outline is developed. As a lesson, this workshop is long and requires extended uninterrupted time. It marks the beginning of the end of the time period allotted for the research portion of the project. Students are completing their research notes—or at least they think they are completing the notes. Students will soon learn (see Workshop 15) as they organize the research note cards into an outline that holes may appear in the researched information. To begin, however, the research note cards must be organized.

Several years ago a seminal article was published in library and information science literature, written by a Canadian library scholar. Titled "Berry Picking" (Bates, 1989), the white paper explored and illuminated the apparent randomness of humans as they choose from vast arrays of new information. The paper essentially explained the particularities of information choice, vis-à-vis the metaphor of picking blueberries in a blueberry bush patch.

The first individual chooses the berries he will pick by criteria that are meaningful only to him. The second person picking berries right next to the first berry picker will choose berries by criteria that are meaningful only to her and may thus move to an entirely different bush. Such, the paper posits, is the nature of the information hunt. Two students researching the same topic will choose different pieces of information depending upon what is meaningful to each individual student.

At this time students are asked to spread out at work tables or on the floor. Each student will need about three feet of space. With the berry picking analogy in mind, students are asked to pull out their research notes and, one by one, read each card with a pencil in hand. Because each card only holds information about one idea, the student is asked to interrogate the card with the following question: "What in general is this card about?" The one- or two-word answer to that question should be written in pencil on the upper right hand corner of the card. The student has now named his first card. He should then rather quickly (do not allow students to belabor the naming) continue to name all the note cards made for the research project. Most students should have between 40 and 50 note cards filled out and named at the end of the exercise.

Once the cards are all named, the student should go through the cards and sort them into piles of like names. For example, the student who is researching Ben and Jerry's Ice Cream might have a pile of cards about the origins of the company, another pile of cards named special flavors, and a third pile of cards about current ownership of the company. Now comes an interesting phase for the student and the teacher. Looking around, the teacher sees that most students each have three to five piles of cards, indicating that the researcher's mind has had its say in determining the meaningful subtopics within the bigger research topic.

For the student who might have more than three piles of cards, ask the student to look at the names on the piles. Are any similar? Can the similar piles be combined under a larger or more general name? If so, the student should combine piles and rename the combined piles by putting the more general name on the top right hand corner above the first name. Students with six or more piles may need help re-sorting and renaming the piles to reduce the number of piles to three (see Workshop 18, "How to Give a Formal Speech"), to provide for more generalized subtopics.

See the illustration below for renaming the card.

Puglisi	**Managing Money** (Main topic)
	Living at Home (Subtopic)

Many young people move back home after completing college in order to save enough money to be able to live on their own. (Paraphrased note)

Growing Up
Page 8

After all students have the cards sorted into three piles, with cards in each pile sharing the same name, the student should then take the first pile, and interrogate each card with the following question:

"What, in relation to the main topic name of this pile, is this particular card about?" That card name of one or two words should be placed under the larger name. Each card in the first pile should be thus interrogated and subnamed. After all the cards in one pile are subnamed, the cards in the second pile should be subnamed and then the third pile should also be completed.

After all the cards in all piles have been subnamed, the student must decide the order of the presentation of the information. Which pile will be presented first, second, and last? When that order is decided by the student, attention must be given to the individual cards within each pile.

The students should place cards with the same subname together and further distinguish each card in the smaller pile by interrogating the card with the question, "What about the subtopic is this card describing?" The student must now give a more particular name on the card under the main topic name and subtopic name. When this is completed for all cards in the first pile, the student determines the order of presentation for the cards in the first pile.

The student then goes on to name and order for presentation the other two piles. After doing so, and with all three piles of cards in order, a volunteer is called upon to bring his cards to the front of the room to be used as the model for creating the organic, already completely organized outline. The teacher, using the volunteer student's piles of cards, writes the title of the presentation on the board.

Part 2

Creating the Outline of Presentation Notes

Each large pile name becomes one Roman numeral under the title. Using the first pile, divisions of Roman numeral I are the subtopics of the pile A, B, and C, if that many subtopics are named. Under each subtopic are the particular names of individual cards sharing a subtopic name, listed as 1, 2, and 3, in the order the student chooses for presenting. The next pile is addressed as Roman numeral II and treated as the first pile was treated. And finally, the third pile is labeled Roman numeral III and so on.

With the outline completed, the student now has a one sheet, organized plan for a speech about the research completed. However, all is not done yet. In most cases, students will observe "holes" in the outline where not enough information has yet been gleaned from the research. To "fatten up" or bulk up the presentation, a little more research must be completed.

The goal of this workshop, of organizing the notes to create an outline, presents a preview of the presentation notes. The preview determines the length, interest level, and gaps within the spoken version of the existing research notes that have been put into the outline of the preliminary order by the student. Having put the research notes in order, the student is now asked to pair up with his/her study buddy. Each student is asked to read the first 25 of the ordered research cards to his/her buddy. The study buddy must complete three tasks:

1. Time the reading
2. Listen to and critique the content
3. Give suggestions to improve the content

Because the presentation notes have not yet been composed, the student begins to understand that the research notes, although in a raw condition, will form the basis for the speech because, after all, the speech is a presentation of the research each student has accomplished. Suddenly the reason for taking notes on the borrowed information comes into focus as the student grows more aware of the necessity of his scholarship to achieve the content of the presentation. The speech can no longer be viewed as an opinion piece or a student's rambling on a subject of the student's interest. The speech is now a presentation of the totality of the student's scholarship. Generally at this point, sighs of relief are heard among students and their teachers. Progress is being made!

Workshop 14: Organizing Your Research Notes for an Outline

Learning Goals: The goal of this workshop is to help students organize research notes to produce an outline of their presentation.
Location: Library (with worktables and ample, open floor space)
Team: Teacher, Librarian, and Resource Guide
Inquiry Unit: This workshop allows the students opportunities to learn how to name and categorize their note cards to strengthen the development of their research presentation.
Total Time: 50 minutes for organizing notes
               50 minutes for outline

Starter Time: 10 minutes Librarian	Librarian brings in a dish of blueberries and discusses how people choose to pick blueberries from a blueberry patch. Librarian asks students how they would each choose which berries to pick. Librarian makes an analogy that picking out information that is meaningful to students is much like blueberry picking and differs from student to student. Librarian asks students to get out their research note cards.
Worktime Time: 30 minutes Inquiry Community	As students have cards in hand they should spread out on the floor or at tables. Each student needs at least three feet of work space. Librarian distributes Student Handout. Students will name each card as per the instructions in the teacher overview for this workshop.
Reflection Time: 10 minutes	Students will reflect as a class on the difficulty and/or ease of organizing large amounts of information. See Student Handout for questions.
Notes:	Once note cards are named and placed in piles of the same name, then the piles are placed in the order the student wishes to present. The next workshop time can be devoted to writing the outline based upon three main topics, subtopics, and card order (see Part 2 of the Overview.) Teaching Team should evaluate completion of this workshop and extend work into upcoming unstructured workshop times and/or offer outside tutorials for students who will need the extra time and support.

Common Core Standards:	RI.9–10.8. Delineate and evaluate the argument and specific claims in a text, assessing whether the reasoning is valid and the evidence is relevant and sufficient; identify false statements and fallacious reasoning. RI.9–10.10. By the end of grade 9, read and comprehend literary nonfiction in the grade 9–10 text complexity band proficiently, with scaffolding as needed at the high end of the range. W.9–10.5. Develop and strengthen writing as needed by planning, revising, editing, rewriting, or trying a new approach, focusing on addressing what is most significant for a specific purpose and audience. W.9–10.8. Gather relevant information from multiple authoritative print and digital sources, using advanced searches effectively; assess the usefulness of each source in answering the research question; integrate information into the text selectively to maintain the flow of ideas, avoiding plagiarism and following a standard format for citation.

Workshop 14

Student Handout: Organizing Your Research Notes for an Outline

Spread out at work tables. If the class is large, sit on the floor and at work tables. You will need plenty of room to complete this lesson. Use a pencil, not a pen.

1. "What, in general, is each note card about?" Name each card.

    Write a general topic name on the upper right corner of card.

2. After naming each card, put in piles by like name.

    • If you have multiple piles, combine those that are similar or related.

    • Try to combine to reach three piles—if you have four or five piles, combine like piles. Try to get down to three general topic piles. Ask for help if needed.

3. Organize the main piles in progression as you think the information should be presented.

4. Within each pile, write a one- or two-word name for each subtopic on the upper right corner of the card under each main topic.

5. Order subtopics within each pile. Order how would you like to present the information, as you think it should flow.

Form the main piles and subtopic piles into an outline. Your three main piles are your three main outline topics, and your subpiles are your subtopics.

Many of you are unsure of how to organize your interview question answers. Interview question answers should not be grouped as an interview. Consider the content of each interview note card and organize it according to that content, just as you organize other cards from other sources by topic/subtopic content.

A brief class discussion may include a statement asking: "How or why did we only end up with three piles each?"

These are some answers that may be given by students:

• "I've picked things that are meaningful to me."

• "I have a 'mental filing cabinet'—my brain picks certain topics."

• "I sort subconsciously—and choose only certain things."

• "That is what I wanted to learn."

Ideally, it is beneficial to write out the card topics as an outline. This outline has already been created organically by piles/subtopics without really thinking about it.

Now, take a blank card and list holes in your outline for later backdoor research. Place card in your research folder.

Workshop 15

Overview: Judging Your Research Notes and Looking for Gaps

Today's workshop marks the beginning of active, real-time preparation for the final presentation of research that each student must make. The presentation is now just three short weeks away and preparations will consume most workshop time from this point forward. The goal of this workshop is judgment of the research note cards to determine whether the student has enough information for a five-minute presentation and whether that information is complete or contains gaps. A secondary, although very important goal is to determine whether the information will make an interesting presentation or whether it is dull and needs to be livened up.

The student's job in this workshop is to review her research notes for the first time and begin to prepare to write presentation notes. The study buddy is an essential element of this workshop because the study buddy is the judge of the notes and will help the student determine the gaps in research findings. Gaps in research mean that the student does not have enough information in one of the three main topics or in one or two of her subtopics. Research note cards may not provide enough content to make a meaningful statement. A gap can be filled or the subtopic eliminated. The student will now begin to judge the research notes.

After the study buddy has listened, made notes, and discussed his judgment of the notes, the first student must reciprocate and do the same for him. The final step in this process will come when study buddies join inquiry groups and each person will read part of his or her research notes to the inquiry group for their feedback.

In this workshop, the relationships developed between study buddies and within inquiry groups are essential to helping each student time and improve the presentation of material. Thus, upon hearing the teacher's instructions and reading the workshop handouts, students must turn to each other for assistance and ideas to improve the individual presentations and ensure audience interest and involvement in the presentation.

The last part of the workshop can be devoted to the whole class's reflection on helping one another better the presentations.

The process of organizing notes and judging what will finally be the speech can be somewhat confusing at first for the student. In many cases the student realizes he has collected enough research to give a very lengthy report, but he knows students are only permitted to present a five-minute speech. So, how does he determine what to include and what to leave out? Here it is beneficial to reintroduce the role of the study buddy. The study buddy is "the audience" and should be encouraged to tell the partner what "stuff" he thinks is "cool" or interesting and what is not. However, the student, not his or her study buddy, is the final judge.

Workshop 15: Judging Your Research Notes and Looking for Gaps

Learning Goals: The goal of this workshop is to provide the students time and space to judge their peers' note cards for sufficient content and coverage and also to judge the interest level of the content.

Location: Library

Team: Teacher, Librarian, and Resource Guide

Inquiry Unit: This workshop is a midpoint within the unit provided to evaluate quality of notes gathered, and to plan final research gathering.

Total Time: 50 minutes

Starter Time: 10 minutes Inquiry Community	Teacher distributes Student Handout to read aloud. Teacher and librarian ask for two student volunteers to get up in front of the class and read each of his/her first 15 notes.
Worktime Time: 35 minutes Study Buddy and Inquiry Community	Students pair up with their study buddy to read *all* of the notes that have been organized and for which an outline has been made. Each study buddy should judge her partner's notes for content and for gaps in the information. The study buddy should also make suggestions how to improve the content if needed. For 15 minutes the inquiry groups will meet to give suggestions to each other of possible changes, additions, or strategies to improve the presentation (see three tasks on Student Handout).
Reflection Time: 5 minutes Inquiry Community	The last five minutes will be devoted to the class reflecting on helping each other.
Notes:	Teacher should emphasize to the students the real responsibility they have to their respective study buddies to help improve each presentation. That responsibility may result in credit added or taken away from the study buddy's final grade.

Common Core Standards:	SL.9–10.1. Initiate and participate effectively in a range of collaborative discussions (one-on-one, in groups, and teacher led) with diverse partners on grade 9–10 topics, texts, and issues, building on others' ideas and expressing their own clearly and persuasively.
	  • Come to discussions prepared, having read and researched material under study; explicitly draw on that preparation by referring to evidence from texts and other research on the topic or issue to stimulate a thoughtful, well-reasoned exchange of ideas.
	  • Work with peers to set rules for collegial discussions and decision making (e.g., informal consensus, taking votes on key issues, presentation of alternate views), clear goals and deadlines, and individual roles as needed.

Workshop 15

Student Handout: Judging Your Research Notes and Looking for Gaps

Today (after having initially organized your 40–45 note cards), you are going to read them to your study buddy.

You and your study buddy will spend the first part of the workshop together doing three tasks:

Task 1: Time your note card reading to determine how much time your presentation will take. You will read to your study buddy your complete set of research notes as you have put them in order to be presented. This order of presentation should be reflected in the outline that you have prepared. Therefore, you should have three main topics under the title of your presentation. Under each of those three main topics you should have two to four subtopics. All of those subtopics should have at least one card of research notes. Your study buddy should time your reading, beginning with the first note and ending with the last. You are trying to prepare a five-minute presentation, no more than five minutes!

Do not be alarmed if you are way over the time limit. This happens to many students. Do not worry if you are having trouble cutting down your note cards because you will have plenty of assistance from your study buddy, inquiry group, and teachers.

Task 2: Determine the "holes" or information gaps in your notes so that you can later fill them in. Your study buddy should tell you whether your information makes sense and has a flow, and where the gaps are in your research. Generally speaking, gaps occur when you do not have enough information to develop a subtopic. A gap can be filled with more research, or the subtopic can be dropped from the presentation.

Do not be discouraged if you have multiple gaps. As long as you acknowledge them at this point in the project, you have plenty of time to fill them in or drop that subtopic. Gaps are a natural part of the research process.

Task 3: Determine whether your notes for your speech are dull or interesting, so that you can liven them up with some backdoor research later this week. Your study buddy should give you suggestions based upon whether your research is interesting and/or lively, whether it is confusing or incomplete, and whether you should add or subtract information to make the presentation whole. Your study buddy is your peer. Your audience for the presentation will be 80 of your peers. You are writing your presentation so that your peers will listen. Remember that.

Remember also, the third task of determining whether the material is dull or interesting comes with a great responsibility because next week, after all the research is complete, if you give a "dull" reading of your research, your study buddy will be penalized one point for lack of due diligence.

Do not be afraid to get a second opinion. If your study buddy wants to cut out something you really like, take advantage of all of those around you who are willing to help and simply ask for another opinion. Ask the other people in your inquiry group.

After your study buddy has heard, timed, and made suggestions about your organized research notes, gather in your inquiry groups to listen to the first half of one another's notes, soon to become speeches, and make further suggestions.

The last five minutes of class will be devoted to the whole class reflecting on what was learned by critiquing each other.

Workshop 16

Overview: How to Do Backdoor Research

The goal of this workshop is to introduce the student to the concept and practice of backdoor research and its place in scholarly pursuits. As the student is reminded, scholarship (or the seeking of information to answer a question or solve a problem) forms a pathway of information from the old information that is searched for and borrowed, to a new idea or knowledge that is gained from combining borrowed information with one's own personal meaning or experience. The student is now transitioning from a searching and gathering mode to a presentation mode, providing his own organization and patterns to the borrowed material and thus beginning the synthesis of ideas. With the transition, the student joins the knowledge gained through research with a learned technique of spoken communication and creates a flow of information in a speech format. As the student begins to put together the speech that presents his research, organizing the research notes will indicate where there are gaps in the information. These gaps call for more research to be completed. Here is where backdoor research becomes necessary.

Backdoor research is a technique a student and scholar will use to fill in the gaps after standard research has been completed. In backdoor research the student searches for unusual, exciting, or tangential information about the research topic by following indirect information paths that may not be obvious approaches but may lead to odd or tantalizing smaller subtopics, which portray the subject in a different light than standard research does.

A graphic example of formal research versus backdoor research is an analogy of a cul-de-sac with several houses on the road. The student is asked to imagine being dropped off at the entrance to the cul-de-sac by a parent one rainy Saturday morning. One of the houses is the house of a new friend with whom the student will spend several hours before being picked up by a parent later on. The student reaches into a pocket and notices that he has neither the address of the friend, Gabe Schmidt, nor his cell phone. Both have fallen out in his parent's car.

The student must now search in the cul-de-sac for the house of his friend by approaching each front door, knocking and in the spirit of the traditional researcher, asking for the information, "Does Gabe Schmidt live here?" After being rejected at several homes, he goes to the second to last home. No one answers the front door. Desperate, the student goes to the backdoor and looks in the window at the cluttered mud room, where he spots his new friend's open book bag spilling over the floor with the same books the student has. Amidst the dirty socks and muddy dog prints on the floor he has found information to lead him to his new friend. The search is over!

Students appreciate the analogy of backdoor research. The librarian can then give a few concrete examples of research topics and how to enliven the topic with some backdoor research. One way to provide examples of subtopics for backdoor research is to call upon a small number of students and ask for the topic each is researching. Any relatively well-read librarian, upon considering the student's topic, should be able to provide the student with some backdoor research subtopic leads, if the student or his study buddy is not able to suggest other possible subtopics. Then let the students go to work, reminding them to look for some additional information about something each has already found tantalizing at the backdoor instead of going to the front door or doing standard research.

Once the backdoor research has been completed and new note cards made, the student may choose to rearrange some of his/her cards for a better presentation. Time should be allotted for such work, should it be needed. When the cards are finally arranged in the days after the back-door research has been completed, students should meet with a study buddy who will be asked to make suggestions about what information to take out if the note card reading is too long. The inquiry groups will be the next people to listen to the first half (2½ minutes) of each set of notes for students in the inquiry group. Time for feedback should be allotted.

Workshop 16: How to Do Backdoor Research

Learning Goals: The goal of this workshop is to introduce students to the concept and practice of backdoor research.

Location: Library

Team: Teacher, Librarian, and Resource Guide

Inquiry Unit: In this workshop students are introduced to a technique for gathering deeper, broader, and/or more interesting information for their presentations.

Total Time: 50 minutes

Starter Time: 20 minutes Inquiry Community	The librarian distributes Student Handout and using the board or projector begins to draw a diagram of a cul-de-sac road with six or seven houses on it, describing the scenario laid out in the overview. Teacher asks for volunteers to discuss information gaps in research that the students have identified while preparing the notes. The teacher and librarian offer suggestions to fill those gaps for individual students (it may be useful to go student-by-student for this exercise, and begin soliciting recommendations from peers).
Worktime Time: 15 minutes Study Buddy and Inquiry Group	Class breaks into study buddy teams or inquiry groups to discuss gaps in research and make suggestions to peers of what information the student might look for to fill gaps and create a more interesting presentation. At this point the Teaching Team will only facilitate to ensure on-task conversations, which will be student led.
Further Worktime: Time: 15 minutes	Students begin to look for more information with the assistance of the Teaching Team.
Notes:	Another unstructured workshop period may be devoted to continuing the backdoor research to fill the gaps and enliven the presentation before the study buddies time the research notes reading and the inquiry groups listen to the first half of each student's note cards.

Common Core Standards:	Anchor Standard 2. Determine central ideas or themes of a text and analyze their development; summarize the key supporting details and ideas.
	W.9–10.8. Gather relevant information from multiple authoritative print and digital sources, using advanced searches effectively; assess the usefulness of each source in answering the research question; integrate information into the text selectively to maintain the flow of ideas, avoiding plagiarism and following a standard format for citation.
	RI.9–10.3. Analyze how the author unfolds an analysis or series of ideas or events, including the order in which the points are made, how they are introduced and developed, and the connections that are drawn between them.
	RI.9–10.8. Delineate and evaluate the argument and specific claims in a text, assessing whether the reasoning is valid and the evidence is relevant and sufficient; identify false statements and fallacious reasoning.

Workshop 16

Student Handout: How to Do Backdoor Research

Research creates an information pathway that is not always straight.

Old information that is borrowed contributes to new knowledge gained from the ideas and concepts the researcher realizes and understands.

Transition From Research > To Presentation

At this point in the Information Search Process, you are experiencing several transitions while handling the borrowed information and thinking about what that information means to the research topic. With most of the actual research completed, you are transitioning from doing research to creating your presentation of that research. You have organized your note cards and must now synthesize that information with what is already in your head—think about what it all means. You must employ writing techniques such as a hook and transition words to the foundation of your borrowed information to create an interesting flow for your speech. You must examine your notes to find gaps in your information and fill those gaps or discard sections of your notes that are skimpy. You must condense some information and prioritize what you have to present in a clear and concise way. In other words, you must make your personal inquiry into a public statement.

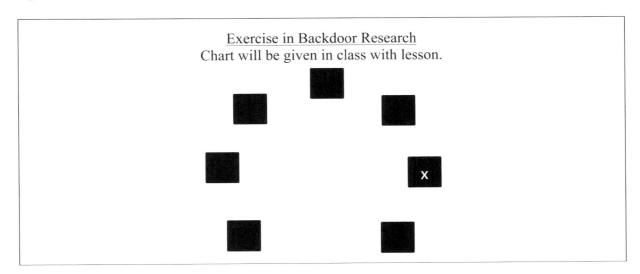

Exercise in Backdoor Research
Chart will be given in class with lesson.

Backdoor researching is a technique a student and scholar will use to fill in the gaps left after regular research has been done. In backdoor research, you are searching for unusual, exciting, or off-beat information about the research topic by following indirect search paths, i.e., "stuff" indirectly related to the research topic—but "stuff" interesting to the researcher. Examples will be given in class.

Research in the Presentation Stage of the Information Search Process

Workshop 17: Using Formal Language and Understanding the Difference
    Between Private and Public Language
Workshop 18: How to Compose Your Presentation Notes
Workshop 19: Audio/Visuals—What Do You Need?
Workshop 20: Using EasyBib to Complete the Bibliography
Workshop 21: Practicing the Presentation

During the Presentation Stage, five workshops and a whole lot of work are scheduled and detailed herein. At this stage, the students' workload may include practicing at home as well as during workshop periods. Care should be taken that presentation notes are not lost. Extra unstructured workshop times must be scheduled for practice and at least one extra unstructured workshop should be scheduled to complete the bibliography.

This period marks the beginning of the Information Search Process coming to fruition. By the end of the time allotted for these five workshops and the multiple rehearsal sessions, the students will express some relief as the presentations of their research findings begin. The presentation stage is a time when full involvement is expected of all students and the Teaching Team becomes full-time coaches.

Workshop 17

Overview: Using Formal Language and Understanding the Difference Between Private and Public Language

The goal of the workshop on formal versus informal language is to enable the student to understand what type of language is used in a public presentation and why it is used. In the digital era, however, the lines between private language and public language have blurred, and students do not often realize or understand what happens to private language when it "goes public," entering the realm of mass or commercial media through social networks. After the workshop, the student should be able to distinguish between the kinds of words and phrases used in public and the kinds of words and phrases used in private, and how and why the public and private words and phrases differ.

The transformation of private language into the public sphere is explained and discussed in the context of how the student should prepare a public presentation to peers.

The workshop is designed using philosopher Hannah Arendt's definition of the public and private spheres found in her book, *The Human Condition* (1958). Students walk away from this workshop knowing that public language should be "formal" and therefore should be more precise, accurate, and guarded. Public language, the student must understand, is not based on shared values, experiences, or understandings. Public language, as used in a presentation, must be utilized and delivered without the speaker assuming the audience has prior knowledge about what the speaker is discussing. Thus public, formal language is delivered without contractions, imprecise pronouns, slang, abbreviations, and typical teen-age jargon such as "like," "um," "ya know," and "yeah." Exceptions to the use of formal language in a public presentation are direct quotations used within the presentation, clearly noted as quotations.

Two good examples to use of the nature of informal language and speech are:

1) A family reunion picnic on the Fourth of July with only extended family, where a favorite uncle tells a story about something embarrassing that occurred while he and your father were young. The familiar story is not even finished before people start laughing and joking because they either were part of the original event or have heard the story before . . . many times. They know nicknames, the symbolic words, and the situation of the story.

2) Students imagine sitting around in a bedroom with one or two other close friends, talking about something funny or silly that happened to them last summer while they were together.

In both examples, the whole story does not have to be told because the story is a shared experience. Laughter and joking ensues as participants interrupt each other, use favorite slang, and finish each other's sentences. The language is informal, including contractions, nicknames, and shared symbolic words.

Differences Between Language in the Private and Public Spheres

Private Sphere   **Public Sphere**

Informal language is private language

Based on shared values, experiences, or understanding.

Formal language is public language

Should be precise, accurate, and guarded because the speaker does not assume shared values, experiences, or understanding.

Realm of commercialized social media for blogs, wikis, etc. and other social networking sites

The kinds of words and phrases used in private are often different from the kinds of words and phrases used in public.

Social media can no longer be considered in the private sphere, even though students still assume it to be private and often use private language addressing friends and social media connections. Social media is now considered to be moving into the public sphere in this culture, even though public regulations about social media may not have been finalized. The illusions of privacy and assumptions that students make about online sharing now fall into the shaded area between the private and public spheres. But for the purposes of communication, of commerce, and of law, language used in social media should be as guarded as in the public sphere.

Workshop 17: Using Formal Language and Understanding the Difference Between Private and Public Language

Learning Goals: The goal of this workshop is to enable the students to understand what language is used in a public presentation and why it is used. At the conclusion of the workshop, students should be able to distinguish between public and private language.

Location: Library

Team: Teacher, Librarian, and Resource Guide

Inquiry Unit: This workshop begins the design of the final presentation.

Total Time: 50 minutes

Starter Time: 15 minutes Inquiry Community	Librarian distributes the handout and asks for a volunteer or volunteers to read aloud to begin this workshop about understanding the difference between private and public language.
Worktime Time: 20 minutes Inquiry Community	After reading the handout together, the librarian introduces the two scenarios found in the Teacher Overview, and/or other similar scenarios. After the scenarios are presented, the librarian asks the students to discuss typical behaviors and language exhibited within those scenarios.
Reflection Time: 15 minutes Inquiry Community	Librarian draws or projects the two intersecting spheres on the board to ask students to reflect on the practices, problems, and issues surrounding language on the social media sites (a Venn diagram can be used for a visual aid, as seen in the handout).
Notes:	While the students may not have often—if ever—considered the difference between public and private language, the social media milieu is increasingly engaging them in the dilemma of these spheres intersecting. This can be used as a teachable moment for discussing the perils and potentials of social media in addition to emphasizing the importance of preparing for a public presentation.
Common Core Standards:	Anchor Standard 4. Produce clear and coherent writing in which the development, organization, and style are appropriate to task, purpose, and audience. W.9–10.5. Develop and strengthen writing as needed by planning, revising, editing, rewriting, or trying a new approach, focusing on addressing what is most significant for a specific purpose and audience. SL.9–10.6. Adapt speech to a variety of contexts and tasks, demonstrating command of formal English when indicated or appropriate.

Workshop 17

Student Handout: Using Formal Language and Understanding the Difference Between Private and Public Language

The modern philosopher Hannah Arendt explains the difference in human behavior within the public and private spheres in her book, *The Human Condition* (1958). As she explains, within the protective private sphere of home and family and friends, certain actions and speech are understood and even tolerated because they are based on shared experiences and values. These actions are relaxed, unguarded, and less disciplined because they stay behind the closed doors of home and within the privacy of family and friends. Private language used with familiar people is informal language. It includes slang, contractions, abbreviations, codes, and shared symbolic meanings. Such language stays in a private setting.

On the other hand, according to Arendt, the public sphere, which includes the marketplace, the political arena, and institutional settings, requires a different approach to and understanding of actions and speech. Within the public sphere, actions and speech/language have more power to affect events and other people and, therefore, should be more precise, accurate, guarded, and formal. In the public sphere, **one must not assume shared values, experiences, or understandings**. Public actions and speech/language must be delivered and explained without the speaker assuming the audience has prior knowledge about what he/she is saying. The modern media and social media is now considered part of the public sphere.

In public one must be careful to speak formally, introducing the subject and being careful that words used will be understood. Formal language avoids contractions, imprecise pronouns, slang, abbreviations that are not explained, and typical informal jargon such as "like," "um," "ya know," and "yeah." **Your public presentation will be given using formal language unless you use a quotation that includes informal language, which you must clearly note.**

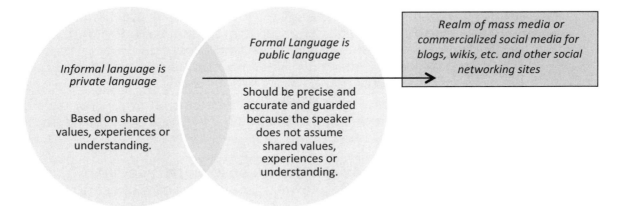

Workshop 18

Overview: How to Compose Your Presentation Notes

It was actually easier for me to pick and choose the information out of my 45 [note cards] then just having to use only 15 note cards for my speech.
— Casey Puglisi, Student, Gill St. Bernard's School, December 2010

The students are reminded that their speeches will be scholarly public presentations of only the findings of their research. Their presentations will *not* be opinion speeches or interpretative speeches. The student is expected to tell the audience what was found when researching the topic. By this point in the preparation for the public presentation, *all* student readings of the presentation should be done at a stand-up podium.

Now the work to create an interesting and lively presentation begins in earnest. The goal of this workshop is the creation of a complete set of presentation notes to be used for the student's actual research presentation to peers and teachers. To begin the workshop, students are introduced to the guest teacher, who is the drama coach. Each student will then receive a handout titled, "How to Give a Formal Speech," which outlines the drama coach's remarks. The drama coach will give his/her speech.

Students are then asked to break up into study buddy pairs and read each other the updated research notes in the order that the student has decided to present. The study buddy has three jobs during the reading, first to time the reading and second to notice and make notes about mistakes in information and gaps in the material. Last, the study buddy must determine how the flow of the presentation can be improved after hearing and observing the reading of the organized research notes.

After each person has read the research notes to the study buddy and listened to the critique, the student takes the rest of the workshop period to begin writing presentation notes using the transition words or phrases sheet the teacher has handed out. The teacher will also provide a brief explanation about the use of transitions to smooth out the information written onto the presentation notes. (It is expected that each teacher already has materials that explain transitions and provide lists of transition words.)

Note cards for the presentation should be numbered in sequence and either hand written onto 5x8 note cards or word processed and attached to the 5x8 note cards. The student will be giving a speech presentation using these exact cards. Thus, the cards must be legible. This workshop may need two sessions to complete. When the cards are completed, each student should read the first half of his speech to his inquiry group for critique.

If students decide to type up their presentation notes, they will easily be able to edit and move around text. A good idea is to make text boxes in Microsoft Word and measure them to the size of the 5x8 note card so that when the presentation is printed, the students will only have to cut on the lines of the text box.

From *A Guided Inquiry Approach to High School Research* by Randell K. Schmidt. Santa Barbara, CA: Libraries Unlimited.
Copyright © 2013.

Workshop 18: How to Compose Your Presentation Notes

Learning Goals: The goal of this workshop is to introduce students to the mechanics of a formal speech. The workshop participants will use student-generated research notes to compose their presentations.

Location: Library

Team: Teacher, Librarian, and Resource Guide (Drama Coach/Theater Teacher)

Inquiry Unit: This workshop develops student notes from previous workshops, and provides a format and expectations for creating and delivering presentation notes into a speech.

Total Time: 50 minutes

Starter Time: 20 minutes Resource Guide (Theater Teacher)	Teacher introduces drama coach/theater teacher, who will give a lesson on formal speech making. Handout #1 should be distributed to students before the theater teacher begins. The theater teacher's instructions are outlined in Handout #1.
Worktime Time: 30 minutes Study Buddy	Students, in study buddy teams, will begin to use their research in a three-topic speech, employing lists of transition words to transition from one research note to another when needed. The aim is to compose the presentation notes for the three main topics of the speech and to do so with the assistance of the teacher, librarian, and theater teacher circulating while the students are writing and helping each other. Handout #2 should be distributed to students as they begin these discussions.
Reflection Time:	See Notes below.
Notes:	No reflection time is allotted because this workshop is an intensive experience. Another unstructured workshop time should be allotted for the students to finish their presentation notes.
Common Core Standard:	SL.9–10.4. Present information, findings, and supporting evidence clearly, concisely, and logically such that listeners can follow the line of reasoning and the organization, development, substance, and style are appropriate to purpose, audience, and task. SL.9–10.5. Make strategic use of digital media (e.g., textual, graphical, audio, visual, and interactive elements) in presentations to enhance understanding of findings, reasoning, and evidence and to add interest. SL.9–10.6. Adapt speech to a variety of contexts and tasks, demonstrating command of formal English when indicated or appropriate.

Workshop 18

Student Handout #1: How to Give a Formal Speech

Guest Teacher:
Paul Canada, Chair, Fine Arts Department
Public Speaking

"Three Is a Magic Number"—Mr. Canada
Lesson developed by Paul Canada

For introduction:

1. Introduce myself.
2. Topic
   a. First general aspect of my research I will talk about . . .
   b. Second general aspect of my research I will talk about . . .
   c. Third general aspect of my research I will talk about . . .
3. Specifics
   a. State three specific things you will discuss.

Students take time writing out their introductions and sharing them with the rest of the class.

(Mr. Canada imparts advice to students. His brother is a minister, and when preparing sermons he finds it effective to make three points and tell a joke. Students should consider doing the same when writing their speeches.)

When writing a paper or a speech, here is how it should be set up:

A. Introduction: "Tell them what you are going to tell them."
B. Body: "Tell them."
C. Conclusion: "Tell them what you told them."

Other Suggestions:

- Use a hook or a schtick or a joke—capture your audience, actively engage your audience.
- Appearance on presentation day is important. Dress formally (unless you are wearing a costume). Be sure your hair is out of your face.
- Stand up straight.
- No gum chewing.
- Point to poster or realia at appropriate time.

Workshop 18

Student Handout #2: How to Compose Your Presentation Notes

Use the largest note cards (5x8) and number the note cards after you have written them.

1. Decide on your hook. It could be a visual statement such as a costume, prop, or bowl of realia. It could be an audio statement such as spooky noises or beautiful music. It could be an actual statement that is shocking, astounding, or just plain interesting. It could be a joke that illustrates your topic. Write your hook on your first note card if you will be speaking it.

2. Next, take your research note cards in the order you have organized them. Perhaps now you should number your research note cards. Look at your research note card outline.

   To begin your speech, start with your hook, then introduce yourself and tell your audience the title of your talk. Make the title sound lively or interesting. Then list the three main subjects you will discuss. Write all of this on your first big presentation note card.

3. Now, beginning with your first research note card, begin to write your speech on the second big note card. Use transition words when needed from one research note to the next. Write neatly and clearly so you can read what you have written. If you prefer to type the note card, that is fine—*in large type.*

4. If you use a quotation in your speech, be sure to make the quotation marks on your presentation note cards and indicate who said it.

5. After you have presented your three main points, then write a concluding presentation note card retelling your audience what you have presented.

   How to write your Conclusion:

   "In conclusion, I have just reviewed _____, I have talked about _____, _____, and _____ (your three big general topics)."

6. Say thank you and smile. Sit down.

7. You did it—Good Job!

8. **Now practice that speech!!!**

First Card

1. Name your hook—costume, quote (write out), joke (write out), bowl of candy or other realia (describe), etc.

2. Intro: Hello, my name is _____. My speech today is *Title of your presentation.* I will be discussing *Three Main Topics.*

Second Card

Begin writing your speech as it appears on the research card.

If using a quote—identify who said it! Use quotation marks for actual words. You do not want more than four or five quotes in your whole speech.

Workshop 19

Overview: Audio/Visuals—What Do You Need?

In scholarly circles, poster sessions are often incorporated into conferences in which larger groups of people congregate to share and learn about current or ongoing studies involving some field of knowledge. The goal of this workshop is to explain and explore the use of an audio/visual component in a scholarly presentation. While students incorporate other audio/visual aids in the presentation such as the realia of costumes, food, animals, and art objects, each student is also required to produce a poster—either a single panel, bifold, or trifold to illustrate some important aspect of the research project being presented unless he/she has other substantial audio/visuals. In other words, this element of audio/visual aid mimics the real-life research presentation in which the scholar sets forth a preliminary (incomplete) visualization of aspects of current ongoing scholarship in a "poster session" at a scholarly conference.

The audio/visual aid is meant to illustrate some aspect of the student's research in a graphic, pictorial, audio, or tactile fashion that emphasizes a point or captures a concept within the presentation speech. For the neophyte presenter, the poster draws the attention of the audience away from the person presenting and toward the visualization of the material being presented. The poster can serve as an enhancement to the speech. A well-designed and creatively executed poster improves the speech with its added visual dimensions.

However, the designer of the poster should remember that only a part of the speech is highlighted. The poster should be clearly titled with text, pictures, and charts or graphs that are readable from 15 feet away. The student handout on audio/visual aids gives pointers on the poster design.

Other visual aids such as a costume or realia are also encouraged to bring added dimension and interest to the research presentation. If the realia consists of a live animal or food product, special arrangements for relocation of the presentation to an outdoor setting or a cafeteria may be considered.

Students often ask if a video clip can be shown during a presentation. Over the years we have found it difficult to allow multiple speakers to use video, not because such technologies are less illustrative but more in the interest of continuous flow from one presentation to the next and time constraints. Compatibility of video display and projection of images from one project to the next is impossible to ensure—even with prior rehearsal. Time is lost hooking up equipment and retrieving devices. Thus, for the past several years we have disallowed the use of video clips for the presentation.

Audio aids are permitted if the student has an audio accompanist who only works one instrument with one audio clip and who has shown swiftness of dispatch during rehearsal. Other audio/visual aids have been all manners of food (given out after presentation during a break in bite-sized portions), cups of coffee or hot chocolate, automobiles, horses, a sheep, dogs, sports equipment (almost all displayed outside), a fashion show, a Barbie Doll display, and on and on.

When sitting through over 80 five-minute spoken presentations in two school days, the audio/visual aid serves the purposes of keeping the audience focused and the speech illustrated.

Workshop 19: Audio/Visuals—What Do You Need?

Learning Goals: The goal of this workshop is to introduce students to ways in which the use of audio/visual components(s) can enhance a scholarly presentation of research.

Location: Library

Team: Teacher, Librarian, and Resource Guide

Inquiry Unit: This workshop presents and explains examples of audio/visual components, particularly the poster, and allows students to incorporate such components into their own presentations.

Total Time: 50 minutes

Starter Time: 10 minutes Teaching Team	Teaching Team carries in several audio/visual aids in the forms of a costume, posters, and a music CD. Students are informed of the nature of audio/visuals in scholarly work presentations, as described in the overview. The handout is distributed to each student.
Worktime Time: 20 minutes Inquiry Community	In a series of "show and tell" brief presentations, the teacher holds up an audio/visual and asks the students what it represents—What is it highlighting about what subject? The librarian asks students, What is the quality of the poster? Is it visible, neat, creative, and interesting?
Reflection Time: 20 minutes Inquiry Group	Students will meet in inquiry groups to reflect upon the audio/visuals they have just seen or heard and to brainstorm audio/visuals they might employ.
Notes:	Another unstructured workshop time should be allotted to create the individual student's audio/visual. Please note the instructions in the overview about computer-delivered audio/visuals. While students are encouraged to use borrowed audio/visual clips (i.e., CD track or MP3), a poster visual aid should be made. If the Teaching Team has flexibility with time and space allotment for presentation day, students may be allowed to use alternative audio/visual components that require more time to set up and integrate into the presentation. See overview for restrictions.

Common Core Standards:	Anchor Standard 2. Integrate and evaluate information presented in diverse media and formats, including visually, quantitatively, and orally. SL.9–10.4. Present information, findings, and supporting evidence clearly, concisely, and logically such that listeners can follow the line of reasoning and the organization, development, substance, and style are appropriate to purpose, audience, and task. SL.9–10.5. Make strategic use of digital media (e.g., textual, graphical, audio, visual, and interactive elements) in presentations to enhance understanding of findings, reasoning, and evidence and to add interest. SL.9–10.6. Adapt speech to a variety of contexts and tasks, demonstrating command of formal English when indicated or appropriate.

Workshop 19

Student Handout: Audio/Visuals—What Do You Need?

An audio/visual (A/V) is required for your presentation. This is an audio or visual aid that will be used to illustrate a key point or idea. It should illustrate or represent only *part* of your presentation. You may use no more than 30 seconds for your A/V, and if you "borrow" the information, which you probably will, you must cite the borrowed material in your bibliography. An A/V can be a still photo, a recording, or a poster. An A/V can also be a costume or prop, instrumental music, sound effects, or food models.

Posters are required as A/V's for this project unless you have other teacher-approved A/V's or substantial realia. In the world of scholarship and academia, the poster session of a conference often introduces one's peers to a newly researched question or topic. Such posters, unlike the later published study, are used to highlight and call attention to important information found or realized during the research but certainly do not depict all of the research.

Your A/V will be graded and must be handed in during class by _____. Nothing received after this date will be accepted.

Unless directed otherwise, you may not use PowerPoint or any computer-generated or computer-delivered video, especially due to presentation time constraints.

To prepare for your presentation, you should make a card with your name, title of presentation, realia, and primary source listed. Also list what A/V equipment you might need for your presentation and if you need special arrangements for your presentation. For example, are you bringing a dog? Are you bringing in ice cream? Do you need to present with a piano or other musical equipment? This card will be collected by your teacher to plan the presentation program.

Workshop 20

Overview: Using EasyBib to Complete the Bibliography

A Bibliography, Works Cited, or Reference List serves multiple purposes for the student researcher, as: 1) an information pathway, 2) an account for verification, and 3) an indication of lesson fulfillment. Let us examine each purpose.

1) A bibliography as information pathway is the student scholar's indication of the depth and breadth of the research completed. Because the research presentation is a combined report of the findings from several sources, the bibliography lists all of the sources, allowing the reader of the bibliography to glimpse the nature of the research and even, when necessary, re-create all of the research to replicate the study. In this listing, one finds authentication of the student's scholarship and an embodiment of the results of the student's information search.

2) Just as the listing of sources serves to authenticate the information sources, this pathway allows another scholar or reader to verify the research and allows access to examine all sources as per the researcher's interpretation of the findings in the research.

3) The scholarship listed within the bibliography includes all print sources, online sources, multiple media sources, and interviews or experiences undertaken to fulfill the research assignment. Therefore, such a listing of sources should be complete, up to date, and in the style recommended by the high school English department. In most high schools, the style manual used for basic humanities research is the Modern Language Association Style Manual (MLA). Print or online versions of the MLA Style Manual can be purchased or digitally accessed.

In addition, services are available online to do much of the work of putting together the bibliography in proper order according to the MLA. One such service is EasyBib. The school librarian can assist the student in utilizing a bibliographical service.

Workshop 20: Using EasyBib to Complete the Bibliography

Learning Goals: The goal of this workshop is to reintroduce the need for a bibliography in scholarly work and to familiarize students with a bibliography-generating service they may use to complete the information pathway.

Location: Library (with access to computers)

Team: Teacher, Librarian, and Resource Guide

Inquiry Unit: This workshop provides students an opportunity to present their findings in a visual scholarly report of sources.

Total Time: 50 minutes

Starter Time: 10 minutes Librarian	At the beginning of the workshop the librarian asks the students to remove from their research folders printouts of all sources they have found and to gather any books or materials from holding shelves that the student has used. The librarian will then explain three purposes for a bibliography and why a researcher must provide a listing of sources used as per the overview.
Worktime Time: 35 minutes Inquiry Community	Students log on to the computer with their sources. Students are provided the handout, describing an online bibliography service. Students access the site as the librarian walks the class through the process in the computer lab by demonstrating how to use the site on the projector. Teacher and librarians circulate. At the end of the worktime, students save materials for bibliographies online as instructed.
Reflection Time: 5 minutes Inquiry Community	Community comes together for brief Q&A and are informed when the bibliography must be completed and turned in.
Notes:	This workshop may (for reasons of scheduling) occur either before or after the presentations have been completed. Most likely, the workshop will take place after presentations. Some students may require homework time, another unstructured workshop, or individual conferencing time with a member of the Teaching Team.
Common Core Standards:	Anchor Standard 4. Present information, findings, and supporting evidence such that listeners can follow the line of reasoning and the organization, development, and style are appropriate to task, purpose, and audience. W.9–10.8. Gather relevant information from multiple authoritative print and digital sources, using advanced searches effectively; assess the usefulness of each source in answering the research question; integrate information into the text selectively to maintain the flow of ideas, avoiding plagiarism and following a standard format for citation.

Workshop 20

Student Handout: Using EasyBib to Complete the Bibliography

EasyBib is a citation tool for creating Reference Lists (used in APA and Chicago styles) and Works Cited (used in MLA style). It supports MLA, APA, and Chicago/Turabian styles. For many sources, EasyBib will be able to find the information needed for the bibliographic entry. If not, a fill in-the-blank form will allow you to enter the necessary information. EasyBib will then correctly format it per the chosen style. **As always, it is your responsibility to double check that the entry is correct.**

SAVE YOUR COMPLETED BIBLIOGRAPHY TO A PLACE ACCESSIBLE LATER. See #5 below.

To use EasyBib:

From a **computer connected to the school network** go to http://easybib.com.

1. On the upper right hand side of the page is a prompt "Login or Register." Choose Register and fill in the form to create an account. This account information can now be used to access EasyBib from any computer with internet access.
2. Click "Create New Project." Name the project, choose style, click "Create."
3. Under Project name choose "Bibliography." Select type of entry: book, website, database, etc.
4. Use the Autocite option by typing in the article or book title. If EasyBib can find the articles or books matching the title, it will list them. Select the correct one. Double check that the format is correct: "In Print," "Online" or "Online Database." Items that may be missing from the entry are outlined in red. Often this includes the database name and date accessed. Click "Create Citation."
5. After all of the sources are entered, there are several options. The list will be sorted alphabetically regardless of the order entered. The list can be e-mailed, or saved as a Word document or a Google document. The information will remain in EasyBib in the project created.
6. There is an option to cut and paste your bibliography into a Word document. DO NOT use this option. The document will not have proper formatting.

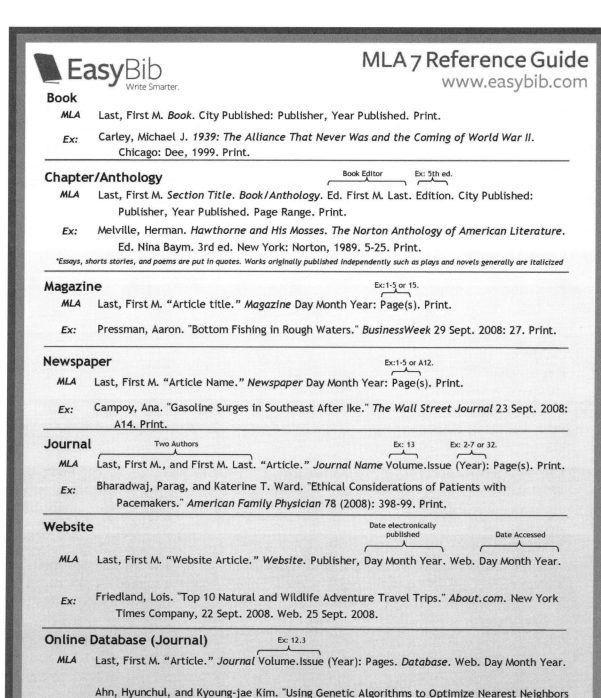

MLA 7 Reference Guide
www.easybib.com

EasyBib Write Smarter.

Book

MLA Last, First M. *Book*. City Published: Publisher, Year Published. Print.

Ex: Carley, Michael J. *1939: The Alliance That Never Was and the Coming of World War II*. Chicago: Dee, 1999. Print.

Chapter/Anthology

Book Editor   Ex: 5th ed.

MLA Last, First M. *Section Title*. *Book/Anthology*. Ed. First M. Last. Edition. City Published: Publisher, Year Published. Page Range. Print.

Ex: Melville, Herman. *Hawthorne and His Mosses*. *The Norton Anthology of American Literature*. Ed. Nina Baym. 3rd ed. New York: Norton, 1989. 5-25. Print.

Essays, shorts stories, and poems are put in quotes. Works originally published independently such as plays and novels generally are italicized

Magazine

Ex:1-5 or 15.

MLA Last, First M. "Article title." *Magazine* Day Month Year: Page(s). Print.

Ex: Pressman, Aaron. "Bottom Fishing in Rough Waters." *BusinessWeek* 29 Sept. 2008: 27. Print.

Newspaper

Ex:1-5 or A12.

MLA Last, First M. "Article Name." *Newspaper* Day Month Year: Page(s). Print.

Ex: Campoy, Ana. "Gasoline Surges in Southeast After Ike." *The Wall Street Journal* 23 Sept. 2008: A14. Print.

Journal

Two Authors   Ex: 13   Ex: 2-7 or 32.

MLA Last, First M., and First M. Last. "Article." *Journal Name* Volume.Issue (Year): Page(s). Print.

Ex: Bharadwaj, Parag, and Katerine T. Ward. "Ethical Considerations of Patients with Pacemakers." *American Family Physician* 78 (2008): 398-99. Print.

Website

Date electronically published   Date Accessed

MLA Last, First M. "Website Article." *Website*. Publisher, Day Month Year. Web. Day Month Year.

Ex: Friedland, Lois. "Top 10 Natural and Wildlife Adventure Travel Trips." *About.com*. New York Times Company, 22 Sept. 2008. Web. 25 Sept. 2008.

Online Database (Journal)

Ex: 12.3

MLA Last, First M. "Article." *Journal* Volume.Issue (Year): Pages. *Database*. Web. Day Month Year.

Ex: Ahn, Hyunchul, and Kyoung-jae Kim. "Using Genetic Algorithms to Optimize Nearest Neighbors for Data Mining." *Annals of Operations Research* 263.1 (2008): 5-18. *Academic Search Premier*. Web. 25 Sept. 2008.

*Note that months in MLA are abbreviated. For example, "February" is "Feb."

YOU CAN ALSO AUTOMATICALLY CITE YOUR SOURCES FOR FREE AT WWW.EASYBIB.COM

From *A Guided Inquiry Approach to High School Research* by Randell K. Schmidt. Santa Barbara, CA: Libraries Unlimited. Copyright © 2013.

MLA 7 Reference Guide
www.easybib.com

TV/ Radio

MLA "Episode." Contributors. *Program*. Network. Call Letter, City, Date. Medium.

Ex: "The Saudi Experience." Prod. Mary Walsh. *Sixty Minutes*. CBS. WCBS, New York, 5 May 2009. Television.

Film

DVD, Film etc..

MLA *Title*. Contributors. Distributor, Year of release. Medium viewed.

Ex: *The Dark Knight*. Dir. Christopher Nolan. Perf. Christian Bale, Heath Ledger, and Aaron Eckhart. Warner Bros., 2008. DVD.

Sound Recording

MP3, CD etc...

MLA Contributors. "Song." *Album*. Band. Manufacturer, Year. Medium.

Ex: Corgan, Billy, and Butch Vig. "Today." *Siamese Dream*. Smashing Pumpkins. Virgins Records America, 1993. CD.

Visual Art / Photograph

MLA Last, First M. *Painting*. Year created. Medium of work. Museum / collection, City.

Ex: Picasso, Pablo. *Three Musicians*. 1921. Oil on panel. Museum of Mod. Art, New York.

Lecture / Speech

MLA Last, First M. "Speech." Meeting / Organization. Location. Date. Description.

Ex: Obama, Barack H. "Inaugural Address." 2009 Presidential Inaugural. Capitol Building Washington. 20 Jan. 2009. Address.

Interview

If any | Magazine, newspaper, television information

MLA Interviewee. "Title." Interview by interviewer. Publication information. Medium.

Ex: Abdul, Paula. Interview by Cynthia McFadden. *Nightline*. ABC. WABC, New York. 23 Apr. 2009. Television.

Cartoon

If any | Magazine, newspaper, book

MLA Last, First M. "Title." Cartoon / Comic strip. Publication information. Medium.

Ex: Trudeau, Garry. "Doonesbury." Comic strip. *New York Times* 8 May 2008: 12. Print.

*Note that months in MLA are abbreviated. For example, "February" is "Feb."

YOU CAN ALSO AUTOMATICALLY CITE YOUR SOURCES FOR FREE AT WWW.EASYBIB.COM

From *A Guided Inquiry Approach to High School Research* by Randell K. Schmidt. Santa Barbara, CA: Libraries Unlimited. Copyright © 2013.

Workshop 21

Overview: Practicing the Presentation

First and foremost this project helped me with my public speaking. It helped me get comfortable with standing up in front of people and speaking, while learning new things and teaching people new things.
                    —Chris Ward, Student, Gill St. Bernard's School, December 2010

Excitement and anticipation are building as we enter the next to last phase of the ISP, which will culminate with each student giving a five-minute presentation of the research completed. During the ten days to one week before the dates set for the presentations, the bulk of the student's work is practicing the oral presentation in front of small groups of peers. To prevent monotone repetition and to ensure listener interest, each student will first read the entire speech to his/her study buddy and then the study buddy will reciprocate. Each will listen to the other and make suggestions to improve delivery of the speech. Each will also time the other to ensure the speech is neither too long nor too short.

Next, practice will resume with the inquiry groups listening to their fellow members, but not to the whole speech; each presenter will only give the first half of their speech. Critiques and suggestions to improve flow will be given by the inquiry group members.

On another day of practice, the entire class can come together. In a random fashion, class members will be called upon by the teacher to read the first third of the speech, the second third, or the final third. The entire class will listen and offer praise and constructive critique.

Another day of practice can begin with each student again meeting with the study buddy to read, time, and rehearse the entire speech. On this particular rehearsal day after the study buddy meeting, the class will rejoin one another to discuss presentation day appearance, costumes, props, and final questions.

A fourth day of rehearsals may consist of full dress rehearsal mode with poster, media, and costume in front of the inquiry group, with each student presenting his entire five-minute speech and teachers circulating for on-the-spot observations.

All of these rehearsals are followed by the last day of logistics. The final schedule of time and location for each presentation is posted publicly for all to note. Posters are collected and placed in sequence in the library. Note cards are scrutinized; costumes and realia are stashed in safe corners of the library office. CD players or iPods are stowed safely. The presentation room with a substantial wooden podium and microphone are set for the big day. The availability of alternate locations are reverified and faculty are reminded of their invitations to observe the presentations. Programs are printed (see Appendix E) and folding chairs for additional seating are put in place. The show is about to begin.

Of course, the above schedule is merely a suggestion. Other arrangements can be made. Please observe at least one week of rehearsals.

With the completion of the research project upon us, I can officially say that the entire process was fascinating. Seeing students struggle through uncharted waters always makes for interesting observations.

Early on, as I witnessed the students' initial efforts I began to make my predictions as to which students were going to succeed and really grasp the concept and which ones were going to have difficulty. For the most part, the students that I predicted would deliver good presentations did not disappoint. They were confident and seemingly prepared and delivered interesting and entertaining information. The real surprises came with the kids who, for many reasons, showed signs of difficulty and stress throughout the preparation. It was those students who were able to find their "five minutes of fame" in some truly wonderful speeches. These students, who seemed so nervous and unsure in rehearsal, came through with flying colors during performance. In some cases the success may have been due to the pure human "fight or flight" instinct that allows people the ability to rise to an occasion under pressure. But in other cases it was simply the fact that they could be surrounded by a familiar and comfortable environment such as a field, corral, cafe, patio, or even a big tree that gave them the confidence to speak clearly and eloquently about their topic.

With projects of this magnitude, I always find it fantastic to see which students rise to meet the grandeur of the occasion and which ones allow the occasion to overpower them. For the most part, the vast majority of students will rise up and seize the moment delivering a commendable product. For the small minority of students who just "don't get it," I imagine no amount of enthusiastic instruction would have changed their outcome. However, even the slightly less than stellar final products proved to be a good learning tool for others.

—Margery Schiesswohl, Seminar Teacher, Gill St. Bernard's School, May 2012

Workshop 21

Student Handout: Presentation Instructions

I. Appearance

    A. Unless you are dressing in character, you must dress nicely for a formal speech.

    B. No gum chewing.

    C. Hair out of your face—we mean it!

II. How to Organize your Speech

    A. Introduce yourself.

    B. Introduce your topic.

    C. Tell 'em what you are going to tell 'em.

    D. Tell 'em what is in your note cards.

    E. Tell 'em what you told 'em.

III. Other Things to Remember

    A. Write narrative (as if speaking) on large cards, 5x8, using complete sentences from your research notes.

    B. Hook: Grabs the audience's attention.

    C. Use something from your primary source in your speech presentation.

    D. Audio/Visual

        1. If you are using a poster or any other A/V, refer to it in your speech to illustrate a point.

        2. Use only 30 seconds or less of A/V.

    E. Use transitional words or phrases between the various points and sections of your speech.

IV. Closing. At the end of your presentation your audience should be able to answer at least the majority of these questions: WHO, WHAT, WHERE, WHEN, WHY, AND HOW?

Research in the Assessment Stage of the Information Search Process

Workshop 22: Essay to Reflect on Your Learning: "What Did I Learn About Myself?"

During the Assessment Stage, only Workshop 22 "Essay to Reflect on Your Learning: 'What Did I Learn About Myself?'" is scheduled and detailed herein. During this period, however, other evaluations continue. For example, the presentation is judged, the students choose the best peer presentation, and the students indicate their three "likes" and three "dislikes" about the entire project. For the essay, one workshop period should be sufficient, but we leave that to the discretion of the Teaching Team, because the students may produce a handwritten draft in the workshop, but the teacher may request a corrected, word-processed document for the final copy. The Teaching Team may also schedule a workshop time for a final, in-depth reflection and discussion of the entire Information Search Process and the guided inquiry experience.

Workshop 22

Overview: Essay to Reflect on Your Learning: "What Did I Learn About Myself?"

The goal of this workshop is the in-class production of a two-page, handwritten essay entitled, "What Did I Learn About Myself While Doing My Research Project." The student should be informed that he/she has just completed a guided inquiry project and be reminded that the essay is *not* about what the student learned about the research topic. Instead, the essay is a reflection by the student about the research process and what insights and self-knowledge the student gained while engaging in the guided inquiry, which involved all of the research and culminated in the presentation. Because the essay is done in class, students are given paper on which to handwrite the essay. The student who chooses to may use a computer to word process the essay. The essay is expected to be about 400 words long. One workshop time is allotted for this essay.

Over the years we have assigned this in-class essay to each freshman upon the completion of the research project. Students' responses are graded for sincerity and a deepening critical understanding of the role of the student in his own education. We have received some wonderful essays. Below is an excerpt from one of them:

> I am a new Rob Berman! This project has changed me, for the better! I did activities that I liked and activities that I didn't like. At first, I thought this project was a joke, and it would be very easy. I was wrong. This project made me work hard for that moment right after I finished so I could say, "I worked hard, and I did well."
>
> I learned many things about myself. The helpful teachers and aids taught me better research skills than what I had, better habits like scheduling and editing. Also, now I know that I am capable of researching a topic I know nothing about and in the end, acting like a pro sumo wrestler.
>
> I chose sumo wrestling because I knew nothing about it. I wanted to learn about it, and sumo wrestling was a fascinating topic to me. At first, the research started slow and the notecards were a nightmare; however, I persevered through the tough times and had a fabulous time. I learned that I have it in me to take a project by the horns and attack it. My time watching and presenting were great and I am glad I went through this process.
>
> —Robert Berman, Student, Gill St. Bernard's School, May 2012

Workshop 22

Student Handout: Essay to Reflect on Your Learning: "What Did I Learn About Myself?"

We are asking you to write one final essay entitled, "What Did I Learn About Myself?" as you undertook your own research project. Your grade for this paper will be determined by your honesty and the examples and details you give to illustrate what you have learned. *We do not want you to write about your research topic.* We want you to describe some of what you were thinking and how you were feeling while you did the *whole* project. We understand that your thoughts and feelings may have changed during the information search process. *Describe* this to us.

The handwritten paper will be two sides of one legal-sized sheet of paper we will distribute to you in class. If you would prefer to use a computer to word process this document, you may do so. The essay will be written during your last workshop for the Research and Writing Project. *You will be rewarded with a cookie!*

Thanks for the memories of a job well done!!!

Best Regards,

Your Teachers and Librarians,
Your Guides in Research

Appendices

Appendix A

Sample Course Outline
Explanation of the Curriculum

Introduction to the Research and Writing Project
Fall Semester

Instructors: **Mrs. Schmidt, Ms. Puglisi, and Ms. Giordano**

Introduction:

The Research and Writing Project can be viewed as a guide to "How to Survive and Thrive in High School." The class will teach the skills necessary to function and achieve a personal level of success in high school academic work.

Ideally to prepare students for high school work, the research and writing project should be conducted during the fall semester.

The Research and Writing Project Component:

The focus of the Research and Writing Project is the communication of information that has been researched. The reason humans communicate is to share information. Such sharing comes in various forms, but two of the most common are oral presentation and written work. In order to facilitate the qualitative sharing of information in a timely, authoritative, and verifiable manner, research is often necessary. This project serves as an introduction to the elements of research and writing that a student will use throughout high school and in college.

Because information seeking and sharing can be both fulfilling and frustrating, the aim of this project is to engage students in a process of information seeking and sharing that is interesting to each individual and that will answer a personal inquiry each student formulates. The two goals of the project are: 1) to learn how to undertake research as a process of information acquisition, assessment, and assimilation; and 2) to present research findings in oral and written forms that can be shared and discussed for their content and presentation values.

Objectives for the Inquiry-Based Research and Writing Project include:

- Learning to browse through multiple sources
- Choosing a topic that interests and engages the student
- Understanding and writing a description of a personal learning style
- Developing a proposal for the project
- Using multiple sources in varied formats to find diverse information and perspectives
- Preparing research notes from the aforementioned sources
- Preparing a bibliography of sources

- Developing a set of presentation notes
- Preparing an audio/visual aid to highlight portion(s) of the presentation
- Delivering an oral presentation of the research project
- Preparing a written narrative of the research process and what was learned

Required Readings and Materials:

- This textbook contains all materials in a workshop format with lesson handouts.
- The librarians may assign and distribute other pertinent handouts and readings prior to some workshops. These short, one- to two-page readings are required and will be reviewed in class.
- The student will be required to keep all research materials, notes, and handouts in a folder given to him/her the first day of class.
- Most work will be done during class periods.
- Very little homework will be expected. Student research folders will be kept in the library.
- *The student must not lose the folder. It will be collected at the time of the presentations. All materials must be held within the folder, including all borrowed information, print-outs, and note cards.*

Synopsis of the Inquiry:

The Research and Writing Project consists of two components: research and writing, both of which will prepare the student for the types of scholarly work necessary for a successful academic career. We conduct this project as a guided inquiry.

For three or four weekly class meetings the student will meet in the library to research **a topic of the student's own choosing that the student wishes to learn about**. Yes, that is correct: the student gets to research whatever topic he/she chooses based on a question or controversy. The student asks the question. The teacher and librarian guide the student through the search. During the research project the student will learn not only about the chosen topic but also how to access information in different formats, how to determine whether that information is useful, how to combine different sources of information, how to organize what has been found, and how to present the borrowed information. All of these "how to's" involve information choices that the student will make. In other words, **the student will learn to be a high school scholar**.

While the student is learning how to handle all of this new information, he/she will learn how to write about the research. The students will be taught how to write a research proposal, how to keep research notes, how to write presentation notes, how to compose a presentation speech, and how to write a reflection about what the student has learned as a researcher.

A NOTE FOR THE STUDENT

Although this may sound like a great deal of work, the good news is **that most of it will be done in class**. **This project does not require much homework**. However, you must do the work assigned in class. **If you do not do the work diligently, you will receive low or no points for effort.** The other good news is that you will have a whole lot of support, including three teachers and a study buddy.

The Research and Writing Project meets three or four times per week for classes held primarily in the library. The project introduces you to the Information Search Process and guides you on a **research journey of a topic that you choose**. This journey will culminate in a five-minute presentation of your research to your peers.

Keep all information in your folder and leave it in the library in a designated spot. You will use it *every day* of class until the conclusion of the project. *****Remember**: *Research something you are curious about, not something that you know everything about—it will make the project more interesting and easier as well.* All elements of the project will be explained in workshop format several days before the due date for that element. Almost all of your work for this project will be done during class time.

Your research folder is like a traveler's suitcase—in it will be placed all handouts, copies of printouts, work, and notes that you have for your research. Your folder will eventually contain all the souvenirs of your research journey. You and your teachers will be able to chart your progress as your folder fills up.

Appendix B

First, Second, and Third Instruments

The instruments are part of the assessment package SLIM developed by Rutgers University Professors Ross Todd, Carol Kuhlthau, and Jannica Heinstrom (2005) to gauge the accumulation of knowledge and the involvement in research by students as they experience the Information Search Process during a guided inquiry project. Administered at the points when: 1) the student first decides upon a topic, 2) in the middle of the note-taking task, and 3) when presentations have been completed, the three instruments, which are virtually the same, are examined for the progression of knowledge and the accumulation and response to that knowledge, as reflected in the answers of the students. The instruments have, throughout the years, provided a highly effective snapshot of the student's position in the Guided Inquiry. Taken in progression, the instruments have also provided our teachers with measurable assessment of effectiveness of their guidance of the young researchers.

Students should be informed that a questionnaire is sometimes called an "instrument." It is a tool used to measure knowledge, beliefs, or behavior.

We tell the students:

Today you are filling out the first, second, or third instrument (questionnaire) about your research project. We are giving you most of the period to answer just a few questions.

We expect you to answer the questions honestly and sincerely. We are not grading the answers because the answers are your opinions, but we will give you the maximum number of points (20) if you give the questionnaire your best effort. Your teacher will collect the questionnaire before class is over.

Teacher's Note:
The three instruments have each been reduced from two pages to a one-sided page, which may not allow enough space for comprehensive student responses. They can be transferred to two-page documents.

Instrument #1

Class _____   Teacher _____

Name _____   Date _____

Write the title that best describes your research topic at this time:

_____
_____
_____
_____

Your task:

Take some time to think about your chosen topic. Now write down what you know about this topic. When you write down your ideas, use as many words, phrases, and sentences that come to mind that show what you know about your topic.

_____
_____
_____
_____
_____
_____
_____
_____
_____
_____
_____
_____
_____
_____
_____

Why have you chosen this topic? _____

_____
_____
_____
_____

Describe how much you think you know about this topic: Expert Knowledge ( )
Know a Lot ( )   Know Some Stuff ( )   Know a Little ( )   Know Nothing at All ( )

Write down what you think you will enjoy the *most* about researching your topic:

_____
_____
_____
_____
_____

Write down what you think you will enjoy the *least* about researching your topic:

_____

_____

_____

_____

_____

_____

How are you feeling about your project? Why?

_____

_____

_____

_____

_____

_____

_____

_____

Instrument #2

Class _____   Teacher _____

Name _____   Date _____

Write the title that best describes your research topic at this time, midpoint in your research:

_____
_____
_____
_____

Your task:

Take some time to think about your chosen topic. Now write down what you now know about this topic. When you write down your ideas, use as many words, phrases, and sentences that come to mind that show what you know about your topic.

_____
_____
_____
_____
_____
_____
_____
_____
_____
_____
_____
_____
_____
_____

Why have you chosen this topic? _____

_____
_____
_____
_____
_____
_____
_____

Describe how much you think you know about this topic: Expert Knowledge ( )
Know a Lot ( )   Know Some Stuff ( )   Know a Little ( )   Know Nothing at All ( )

Write down what you think you are enjoying the *most* about researching your topic:

_____
_____
_____
_____
_____
_____
_____

Write down what you are enjoying the *least* about researching your topic:

_____
_____
_____
_____
_____
_____
_____

How are you feeling about your project? Why? _____

_____
_____
_____
_____
_____

Instrument #3

Class _____   Teacher _____

Name _____   Date _____

Write the title that best described your research topic at the time of your presentation:

....

....

....

Your task:

Take some time to think about your chosen topic. Now write down what you now know about this topic. When you write down your ideas, use as many words, phrases, and sentences that come to mind that show what you know about your topic.

_____

_____

_____

_____

_____

_____

_____

_____

_____

_____

_____

_____

_____

_____

_____

_____

Why did you choose this topic? _____

_____

_____

_____

_____

_____

_____

Describe how much you now think you know about this topic: Expert Knowledge ( )
Know a Lot ( )   Know Some Stuff ( )   Know a Little ( )   Know Nothing at All ( )

Write down what you enjoyed the *most* about researching your topic:

_____

_____

_____

_____

_____

_____

_____

_____

Write down what you enjoyed the *least* about researching your topic:

_____

_____

_____

_____

_____

_____

_____

_____

How are you feeling about your project now? Why? _____

_____

_____

_____

_____

_____

_____

Appendix C

Letter Sent Home in Preparation for Student Presentations

Each year, three weeks before the presentation days, a letter is sent to parents informing them of the upcoming two-day festival of presentations and asking their support to ensure few absences and appropriate dress for the occasion. With 80 five-minute presentations all booked well in advance, attendance is paramount. Other faculty (because they do not teach students making their presentations on the two days) are cordially invited to the presentations.

The parent letter is below:

November 26, 2012

Dear Parents,

We are delighted to announce that on *Monday and Tuesday (December 17 and December 18)*, all students enrolled in the Research and Writing Program will deliver their presentations to peers, faculty, and a panel of judges. The students have been working diligently, and faculty and students are looking forward to an exciting two days. The topics this year are varied and interesting, ranging from "Ben and Jerry's Ice Cream" to "Werewolves." After much practice, we anticipate some notable performances. It has been our pleasure over the years to see topics (and researchers!) grow and develop.

We want to make you aware of a few guidelines that have been established for presentation days. No student can be absent on Monday or Tuesday without a doctor's written excuse. Students should be appropriately dressed for the formal presentation. Some will wear costumes to highlight a portion of their presentations. Otherwise, proper, neat, and clean attire is expected as each student will be presenting a formal speech. Hair must be neat and off the face. Unfortunately, due to space limitation, parents are asked to help their children rehearse at home but not attend the presentations. If you have questions or concerns, please do not hesitate to contact us.

Sincerely,

Randell Schmidt, Head Librarian

Appendix D

The Appeal of the Research and Writing Program

To call Gill St. Bernard's (GSB) Research and Writing Program comprehensive would be an understatement. Before even writing a single paragraph, students are taught research and note-taking techniques and shortcuts that maximize effective use of time. Students are given a short list of five or six questions to consider when reading through any source. This way, they read with a *purpose*. Furthermore, taking notes in margins and using different color highlighters are only one way in which naïve freshmen become savvy researchers.

Patience is a key attribute held by every member of GSB's library staff. To help offset the tedium with which students must comb through primary and secondary sources, the librarians spend countless hours working one-on-one with *every* student. Their goal is to provide support and direction through the Information Search Process, while allowing the student complete freedom regarding topic selection. Such is the nature of guided inquiry. The belief is that students will pursue topics that interest them much more vigorously than topics that fail to connect with them on a personal level.

The librarians understand just how daunting presenting a five-minute speech can be for any high school student. Consequently, they meticulously bridge the gaps between each step in the process, guiding each student from the opening paragraph all the way through the bibliography. The class dives right into the research process freshman year and must craft a five-minute presentation, summarizing all they have learned. This encourages the incorporation of public speaking into the writing and research process. A medium-length paper, written in conjunction with their sophomore English class, is the focus of sophomore year, while junior year culminates with the much longer, more sophisticated, 15-plus-page scientific literature review.

When considering the impact of the research and writing program, one need not look beyond the school's own library staff. A number of former outstanding students have been employed as interns. This not only ensures that the techniques will be taught consistently and effectively, but that those who teach research methods actually believe in everything they are practicing. Interns tend to be former students who felt so strongly about their own GSB research and writing experience that they have been inspired to pursue careers in research and education.

As an admissions officer, you hope that the things you highlight on tours will actually be delivered, once a prospective family's child is enrolled at the school. While the campus, buildings, and classrooms are crucial in selling a school, it is the follow-through that keeps families happy. More and more families are asking about the research and writing curriculum offered by our school, which has made the library a staple on my own campus tours. Just as with current students, librarians faithfully take the time to chat with every visiting family. Randi's passion for her work is not lost on prospective parents, and it is exciting to watch their interest grow as Randi enthusiastically shows off some of her students' finest work.

This is one area in which the research and writing program shines. Her program is as advertised. Recent GSB graduates regularly recount stories of how well they were prepared to effectively write college level papers, and discuss how they were able to *guide their peers* through the process. Like Randi's interns, her past students quickly become the teachers—spreading the good word of guided inquiry wherever they take their talents.

—Brady Becker, Admissions Office, Gill St. Bernard's School, January 2012

Appendix E

Research and Writing Project Presentation Schedule Sample

Time	Presenter	Topic
8:18	Michael	Ford: The Creation of the Universal Car
8:24	Kaitlyn	What to Do When You Say "I Do!"
8:30	Sam	The History of Punching in the Face

Walk from the Todd Quad

to the stream

Time	Presenter	Topic
8:48	Jenna	What Lives Under the Sea?

Return to the Reference Room

Time	Presenter	Topic
9:06	Meg	The Serious Problem of Sea Turtle Extinction
9:12	Gabi	Fear or Nature?
9:18	Jack	The Most Spectacular Sporting Event: The World Cup
9:24	Rob	The Greatest Sport of All Time: Sumo Wrestling!

To the Café

Time	Presenter	Topic
9:36	Stefan	Life Is Sweet
9:42	Katie	M & M's: Changing the Face of Candy
9:48	Ricardo	Got Milk?

BATHROOM BREAKS
Return to the Reference Room

Time	Presenter	Topic
10:42	Isabelle	A Walk Back in Time
10:48	Kaila	You Broke What Record?!?!
10:54	Allie	Spirits are Everywhere
11:00	Ian	Hell's Gate: A Haunting at Bobby Mackey's Music World
11:06	Grace	Cultural Aspects of Superstitions
11:12	Sarah	The Witch Hunt

To the Chapel

Time	Presenter	Topic
11:24	Xauen	The Music of Film: John Williams
11:30	Sandy	Culture in Stephen Sondheim's Music
11:36	Nita	Read Between the Lines: Beyond the Surface
11:42	Bri	Are You Scared Yet?
11:48	Erin	The Lives and Legend of Bonnie and Clyde
11:54	Bri	Alcatraz: Life Behind Bars at the Worst Prison in the World

Return to the Reference Room

Time	Presenter	Topic
12:06	Corinne	Tiaras and Tears: The Secret World of Child Beauty Pageants

12:12	Mary	Chautauqua: An American Utopia
12:18	Soraya	A Journey into the Ship of Dreams
12:24	Shane	Operation Overlord and the Invasion of Normandy
12:30	Jordan	The Intimidating Fighting Falcon
12:36	Michael	That Others May Live

LUNCH

Seated in the Reference Room by 1:25

1:30	Gunnar	The Birthplace of College Football
1:36	Tyler	Like Mike
1:42	Ethan	Breaking the Ice: Willie O'Ree
1:48	Alex	Look; Don't Touch
1:54	Sam	Subliminal Advertising: Turning Consumers into Zombies

To the Cafe

2:06	Harrison	Colonel Sanders: One Man Behind KFC
2:12	Dan	The Fuel of America's Athletes
2:18	Zeel	The Big Success of a Little Treat: The Popularity of Cupcakes

Tuesday

Time	Presenter	Topic
8:18	Tyler	Snow Leopards: A Vanishing Mystery
8:24	Raymark	Tigers: The Real King of the Jungle!
8:30	Emily	Koko the Gorilla: A Conversation with the Unimaginable

Return to the Reference Room

8:42	Hope	Magical Moments with Mickey
8:48	Jamie	Crayons: From Novelty to Necessity
8:54	Lauren	Hello Kitty and the Feline Frenzy
9:00	Saira	The Magic Behind the Doors of Disney
9:06	Andrew	Fun on the Slopes
9:12	Alec	Baltimore Orioles, Irrelevant?
9:18	Alyx	A True Red, White, and Blue Miracle
9:24	Disha	The Wonderful Life Of Walt

| 9:30 | Ivor | Steve Jobs: Professional and Personal Life |

To the Café

9:42	Will	A Look into the World of Chocoholics
9:48	Armani	Halloween: The History of Horror
9:54	Paige	The Sweet Life of Dum Dums
10:00	Erin	Chewy Sugar

Advisory/Meeting time
Return to the Reference Room

11:00	Eliza	The Beatles: From Me to You
11:06	Edward	The Hardware of Rock n' Roll
11:12	Jacob	Metal Mania Becomes Manic Metal: History of Thrash Metal
11:18	Jonathan	The Biology of Memes
11:24	Morgan	Dreaming the Dream
11:30	Madeline	Bug to Butterfly and Beyond
11:36	Ted	You Wouldn't Want to Get Bitten by This!
11:42	Luisa	Minutes with Marilyn
11:48	Anastasia	The Fashion of Elizabeth I

Outside Behind the Theater

12:00	Amanda	Getting to Know the Life of Vampires
12:06	Jack	Werewolves: Fact or Fiction?
12:12	Julien	Big Foot: Fact or Legend?

Return to the Reference Room

12:24	Eric	Gladiators: Heads Will Roll
12:30	John	Lorenzo de Medici: The Original Godfather
12:36	Liz	Pompeii: The Town beneath the Ashes

LUNCH

Seated in the Reference Room by 1:25

1:30	Isabelle	Equitation: The Blood, Sweat, and Tears Behind the Sport
1:36	Jolie	Draft Ponies Throughout the World
1:42	Olivia	Man's Best Friend

To the Café

| 1:54 | Patrik | Gatorade: The Science in Sweat |
| 2:00 | Connor | A Scoop into Ben and Jerry's Ice Cream |

| 2:06 | Casey | The Fizzy and Tasty World Of Coke and Its Pop-Popularity |
| 2:12 | Max | McDonald's Marketing Madness |

PARTY!!!! & CLEAN-UP

Appendix F

Choosing the Best Presentation

Before the audience is dismissed from the presentations, all students are given a 3x5 index card and pencil and asked to record the presenter's name and topic of the best three presentations. The cards are then collected by the librarian or teacher and tallied for the top three presentations.

Then the party begins! An hour or two should be allotted for a celebration of research, which includes food, music, and displays of posters and realia. This is a time for the students to celebrate that the intensive guided inquiry project is completed and recognize the milestone in academia that has been achieved. The results of the votes for the top three presentations can be announced, with a prize of gift certificates for first, second, and third place, at the end of the party.

Appendix G

Noting the Likes and Dislikes of the Project
IT'S ALL ABOUT THE COOKIE!

Teachers and librarians become well acquainted with their students during the course of the Research and Writing Project. While several assessments occur during the project, perhaps the most succinct assessment is completed by the students at the very end of the project.

After the presentations have been completed and the final essay written about what the students have learned about themselves while doing the research project, the students are given a 3x5 index card. The student should not put his/her name on the card. Each student is instructed to write "Likes" on top of one side of the card, then turn the card over and write "Dislikes" on top of the other side of the card.

On the side marked "Likes," students are asked to name three aspects of the entire research and writing project they most enjoyed—from the start (getting the assignment) to the finish (making the presentations and writing the final essay). Anything they most liked can be included. (Here it must be noted that the most frequently mentioned "Like" is the chocolate chip cookie.)

On the side marked "Dislikes" students are asked to indicate the three aspects of the project (from start to finish) that they most disliked. Students are reminded that their answers should be personal, individual responses not a group consensus.

Once the "Likes" and "Dislikes" are noted and tallied, the Teaching Team has spontaneous evidence of success and sometimes failure in the curriculum, and also in other areas of the guided inquiry that need improvement.

Appendix H

Research Presentation Rubric

Student's Name_____

Topic_____

Points Given	Very Good (2 points)	Acceptable (1 point)	Not Acceptable (1/2 point)
<u>Interest</u> Did the speaker present an interesting topic?			
<u>Organization</u> Was the presentation logical and easy to follow?			
<u>Content</u> Did the student incorporate realia & A/V?			
<u>Performance</u> (Hook, speaking skills, eye contact, posture, etc.)			

Extra credit for exceptional job (2 pts.) _____

Time: If under or over 5 minutes, reduce grade 2 pts. _____

Comments: _____
_____
_____
_____
_____

Total grade for Presentation _____

References

Allen, Bryce. (1996). *Information tasks: Toward a user-centered approach to information systems*. San Diego: Academic. Print.

Arendt, Hannah. (1958). *The human condition*. Chicago: University of Chicago. Print.

Bates, Marcia J. (1989). The design of browsing and berrypicking techniques for the online search interface. *Online Information Review, 13*(5): 407–24. Web.

Becker, Brady. (2012) *"The appeal of the research and writing program."* statement. Gill St. Bernard's School, Gladstone. Statement.

Belkin, Nicholas J. (1980). Anomalous states of knowledge as a basis for information retrieval. *Canadian Journal of Information Science*: 133-43. Web.

Berman, Robert. (2012). *"What did I learn about myself?"* statement. Gill St. Bernard's School, Gladstone. Statement.

Canada, Paul. (2012). *"How to give a formal speech" lesson plan*. Gill St. Bernard's School, Gladstone. Lesson Plan.

Carse, James P. (1994). *Breakfast at the Victory: The mysticism of the ordinary experience*. San Francisco: Harper. Print.

Editors of the American Heritage Dictionaries, ed. (2011). *The American heritage dictionary of the English language*. 5th ed. Boston, MA: Houghton Mifflin Harcourt. Print. Copyright © 2011 by Houghton Mifflin Harcourt Publishing Company. Adapted and reproduced by permission from *The American heritage dictionary of the English language, fifth edition*.

"EasyBib." *EasyBib*. (12 July 2012). <http://content.easybib.com/students/citation-guide/mla/quick-guide/>. Web.

Gardner, Howard. (1983). *Frames of mind: The theory of multiple intelligences*. New York: Basic Books. Print.

Gibaldi, Joseph. (2009). *MLA handbook for writers of research papers*. New York: Modern Language Association of America. Print.

Gordon, Emmy. (2010) *"Putting it into a speech."* statement. Gill St. Bernard's School, Gladstone. Statement.

Knaster, Todd. (2011). *Cookies at home with the Culinary Institute of America*. Hoboken, NJ: John Wiley & Sons. Print.

Kuhlthau, Carol C. (2004). *Seeking meaning: A process approach to library and information services*. Westport, CT: Libraries Unlimited. Print.

Kuhlthau, C., Maniotes, Leslie K., & Caspari, Ann K. (2007). *Guided inquiry: Learning in the 21st century*. Westport, CT: Libraries Unlimited. Print.

Lane, Carla. (n.d.) "Gardner's multiple intelligences." *Gardner's Multiple Intelligences*. <http://www.tecweb.org/styles/gardner.html>. Web.

Lieblich, Max. (2010) *"Sorting through information."* statement. Gill St. Bernard's School, Gladstone. Statement.

Parker, Herald. (2010)) *"Feelings of the seminar emotional roller coaster"* statement. Gill St. Bernard's School, Gladstone. Statement.

Puglisi, Casey. (2010) *"Easy to pick and choose information." statement.* Gill St. Bernard's School, Gladstone. Statement.

Rice, Ronald E., McCreadie, Maureen, & Chang, Shan-Ju L. (2001). *Accessing and browsing information and communication.* Cambridge, MA: MIT Press. Print.

Salinger, J. D. (1951). *The catcher in the rye.* Boston: Little, Brown and Company.

Shiesswohl, Margery. (2012). *"Practicing the presentation" statement.* Gill St. Bernard's School, Gladstone. Statement.

Tierney, Amy. (2012). *"The interview process: The original inquiry tool."* Gill St. Bernard's School, Gladstone. Statement.

Todd, R., Kuhlthau, C., & Heinstrom, J. (2005). *School impact library impact measure reflection instruments and scoring guidelines.* Center for International Scholarship in School Libraries at Rutgers University, 12 July 2012. <http://cissl.rutgers.edu/images/stories/docs/slimreflectionsheet.pdf>. Web.

Ward, Chris. (2010) *"Project helped me with my public speaking." statement.* Gill St. Bernard's School, Gladstone. Statement.

Wengel, Laura. (2012). *"What are learning styles?" statement.* Gill St. Bernard's School, Gladstone. Statement.

Index

About the Author

Randell K. Schmidt is Head Librarian at Gill St. Bernard's School in Gladstone, New Jersey. She is the lead author of *Lessons for A Scientific Literature Review: Guiding the Inquiry*, published by Libraries Unlimited in 2008. Her new book is the result of 12 years of collaboration in guided inquiry research projects with ninth grade students. She developed the program to enable students to learn the information search process as they begin secondary school. She holds a BA from Hanover College, a Master of Divinity degree from Princeton Theological Seminary, and a Master of Library Science degree from Rutgers University.